Donald Berry

R.R. #9 P.O. STA.B

Buchanan Rd

Evansville

Indiana

Sat Jan. 17 1948

THE ROAD TO MUSIC

THE ROAD TO
MUSIC

BY

Nicolas Slonimsky

ILLUSTRATED

DODD, MEAD & COMPANY

New York · 1947

PRINTED IN THE UNITED STATES OF AMERICA
BY H. WOLFF, NEW YORK

TO ELECTRA—

AGAINST HER WILL

Foreword

THIS book grew out of articles published several years ago in the *Christian Science Monitor,* on the Children's Page, edited with enlightened discrimination by Mrs. Ethel Ince. The articles evoked gratifying response from *Monitor* readers, adults, adolescents, and children alike.

In one of my articles I have reproduced the full score of a very short piece (it lasts only 19 seconds) by the late Austrian modernist, Anton von Webern. When I sent him a copy of the article, he wrote me: "I am deeply touched that my music appears on the Children's Page. If only grown-ups were like children, free from prejudice against everything new!"

I am entirely in accord with this sentiment. Children are progressive and have a healthy curiosity. So I decided that whatever else I should do with my articles in revising them for publication in book form, I would not talk down to my audience, whether they be children or adults. When I find that a "modernistic" example suits my purpose, I quote it, along with the rules and regulations for traditional music. When I feel like using a polysyllabic word, I use it. There is no condescension in this book. I treat my readers with healthy respect.

I want to thank the publishers of the *Christian Science Monitor* for the permission to use some of the illustrations which appeared in the original articles. And I acknowledge with gratitude the help of Mrs. Mildred Morse, who drew the new illustrations appearing in this book. My affectionate thanks go to my wife, Dorothy Adlow-Slonimsky, who patiently perused the entire manuscript and weeded out not a few things that were disruptive of the continuity.

The Bach limerick in the twelfth chapter and the one about a young lady from Rio in the twentieth chapter are of general currency; the rest of the poetry in the book is of my own concoction.

Igitur eme, lege, fruere.

Nicolas Slonimsky
Boston, December 15, 1946

Contents

ᘒ I ᘒ

The Musical Alphabet

ALL you need to know to understand this book is the alphabet from A to G. All music is made up of these letters. A is the first letter of the alphabet, but in music, C is the most popular letter-note. This is so because the C scale comes out on white keys on the piano, and is the easiest to play, even for those who use the unidigital method of piano playing, and pick out the notes with one finger.

The keyboard of the piano has white keys and black keys. There are seven different white keys, C, D, E, F, G, A, and B, and there are five different black keys, C sharp, D sharp, F sharp, G sharp, and A sharp. The black keys can also be called flats, D flat, E flat, G flat, A flat, and B flat. The nearest black key to the right of a white key is a sharp; the nearest black key to the left of a white key is a flat. So the same black key may be called either a sharp or a flat.

A white key may also be a flat or a sharp, if there is no black key in between. For instance, there is no black key between B and C, or between E and F (look at the keys on your piano to make sure). Therefore, B sharp is C, and C flat is B. F is E sharp, and E is F flat. There are altogether fifty-two white keys on the piano and thirty-six black keys, adding up to eighty-eight keys in all. That is why the jazz players call the piano simply the Eighty-Eight.

Because the musical notes form an alphabet, we can spell words in music, but of course these words must not have any letters after G. Here are a few musically spellable words: Cabbage, Bed, Baggage, Face, Bee, Ace. You can also spell A Bad Egg in musical letter-notes. And the words "See sharp" can be spelled with just one note, C sharp.

Let us compose a piece on one of these musical words. Here is a recipe for the composition of a Cabbage Waltz. Spell out and play C-A-B-B-A-G-E twice over. Then spell it out backwards, E-G-A-B-B-A-C. Then spell it straight once more, C - A - B - B - A - G - E. Add an oom-pah-pah accompaniment in the left hand,

SPELLING PICTURES WITH MUSICAL NOTES

and try it over on your piano. The result will be a rollicking waltz tune.

Musical notes are written down on a music staff with five lines. These notes are placed on the line or between the lines, so that there is room for eleven different notes on a five-line staff: five notes on the lines, four notes between the lines, one note below the first line and one

THE CABBAGE WALTZ

note above the top line. Beyond these limits, we have to add extra lines, below or above the music staff as the case may be. For very high or very low notes, it is more convenient to put the number 8 and a dotted line above the note to show that it is to be played eight keys, that is, an octave higher. If you write the highest note on the piano without the aid of this octave sign, it will have nine extra lines, and will look like some strange bird perched high on a telegraph pole.

Sharps look like the number sign on the typewriter, #, and flats look like little b's. There are also double sharps and double flats. Double sharps are indicated by little x's, and double flats are simply two flats, one after another. A double sharp raises a note twice, so most double sharps are white keys. For instance, G double sharp is the

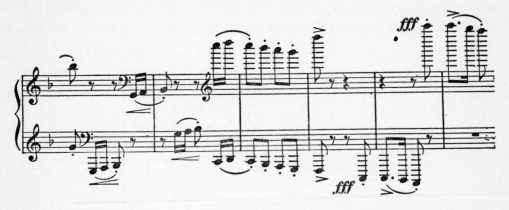

LOW AND HIGH NOTES (FROM *My Toy Balloon*)

same as A. D double sharp is the same as E. Double flats are mostly white keys, too. D double flat is the same as C. I have searched far and wide for a triple sharp or a triple flat, but have failed to find one.

I thought I saw a triple sharp,
    Haranguing from a tree;
I looked again, and found it was
    A humble-looking flea.
Alas! I said, that isn't fair
    To Mr. Chimpanzee.

I thought I saw a triple flat,
    Reposing by the sea;
I looked again, and found it was
    A busy bumblebee.
If this continues very long,
    I never shall drink tea.

In order to cancel a sharp or a flat, you have to put a special sign before the note, a natural sign. If you have to cancel a double flat or a double sharp, you must use two natural signs.

To show which note is which on the music staff, we use clefs. In

French, the word clef means a key. It opens the door to music. The most familiar clef is the G clef, which looks like a fancifully embroidered letter G. The tail of the G clef curls around the second line of the staff to indicate the position for the note G in the middle of the piano keyboard. This G of the G clef is the twenty-eighth white key from the lowest A on the piano keyboard, and it is the twenty-fifth white key down from the highest C. The G clef is sometimes called the Treble Clef, because the high register of musical sounds is named Treble.

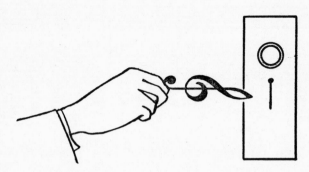

CLEFS OPEN THE DOORS OF MUSIC

For the low register of the musical alphabet, the F clef is used. The F of the F clef is the twentieth white key from the lowest note on the piano, and the thirty-third white key down from the highest. The F clef is also called the Bass Clef, from the word Basso, meaning low, in Italian. Strangely enough, the most familiar note, the middle C, cannot be written without extra lines in either the G clef or the F clef. In the G clef, the middle C will be on an extra line below, and in the Bass Clef, it will be on an extra line above the music staff.

There are also clefs that indicate the position of middle C on the music staff. These clefs are good for melodies that are too low for the G clef and too high for the F clef, quite naturally so, because middle C is exactly in the middle between the G of the G clef and the F of the Bass Clef. If middle C is placed on the third line of the music staff, the clef is called the Alto Clef; if it is on the fourth line, it is the Tenor Clef.

The great name of Bach can be spelled with a single musical note on a crisscross music staff with four clefs to the north, south, east, and west of the note. But the notes must be marked according to German usage, and in the German musical alphabet, our B is H. The Germans also call B flat plain B. The name of Bach will come out in our musical alphabet like this: B flat, A, C, B natural.

BACH SPELLED WITH A SINGLE NOTE

In Italy, France, Spain, and Russia, musical notes are syllables instead of letters. The C major scale runs like this: Do, Re, Mi, Fa, Sol, La, Si, Do, and each syllable is the beginning of a Latin word, as for instance Re for Resound, Mi for Miracle, Fa for Family, Sol for Solve. These syllables are used in a system of notation called the Changeable Do. It is changeable, because Do can be made to be the first note of any scale, the second note being Re, and so forth.

The Interval Hand

THE shortest distance between two points is a straight line, but in music the shortest distance is a semitone. The word semitone means half a tone, just as a semicircle is a half circle. Intervals between E and F and between B and C are semitones. All other intervals between two neighboring white keys are whole tones. Between C and D there is a whole tone, and between D and E, and between F and G, and between G and A, and between A and B.

An octave contains twelve semitones or six whole tones. But in the musical alphabet, in letter-notes or degrees of the scale, an octave has eight notes, C, D, E, F, G, A, B, and C. In fact, the word octave means eighth in Latin. Beyond the octave we have a tenth, an eleventh, a twelfth. The largest interval on the piano is a fifty-second, from the lowest A to the highest C, but of course we do not call it that, but simply say that the piano keyboard has a range of seven octaves and a third, fifty-two notes in all.

Most pianists cannot stretch an interval over the tenth with one hand, but it is said about Bach that he could stretch twelve notes with his left hand, and in addition play trills and tremolos with the three middle fingers. Incidentally, Bach was the first to use the thumb in organ playing. Before him, the use of the thumb was regarded improper, and the organist had to get along with four fingers only. To this day, the thumb is discriminated against by piano teachers who will not allow the thumb to be used on black keys.

Let us write down our musical alphabet like this:

A B C D E F G A B C D E F G A B C

Now let us find the interval of a fifth from A. It is the same as finding the fifth letter of the alphabet, and that is, of course, E. Let us figure out the interval of a fourth from G. Count four letters beginning with G itself—G A B C. C is a fourth from G in musical intervals.

Now let us find a seventh from B. Run over our little alphabet count-ing B as number one. The seventh letter from B will be A. When you count a ninth letter-note, the result will be the same as the second. A tenth will come out the same as a third. A tenth from A is C, and a third from A is also C. A ninth from D is E, and a second from D is also E. It is quite natural that it should be so, because after the octave the musical alphabet repeats itself.

On the music staff, intervals are measured by lines and spaces. If two notes are placed next to one another, one on a line, the other on the next space, looking like two nuts on a stem, the interval is a second. If two notes are both on neighboring lines or neighboring spaces, looking like two balls one on top of the other, then the interval is a third. In all odd-numbered intervals, such as thirds, fifths, sevenths, both notes fall on lines, or both on spaces. In even in-tervals such as seconds, fourths, sixths, octaves, one note comes out on the line and the other on the space. You ought to be able to tell an interval instantly by estimating the distance be-tween two notes, just as you tell the meaning of words in quick read-ing, without actually scanning every letter of each word. An expert musician can read a page of music in semi-darkness, by the shape of the intervals.

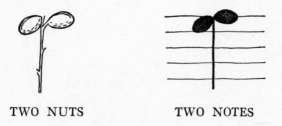

TWO NUTS   TWO NOTES

There are minor and major, augmented and diminished intervals. A minor second has only one semitone, as for instance, A to B flat; a major second has two semitones as for instance, A to B. A minor third has three semitones; a major third has four semitones. There are no major or minor fourths. There is a perfect fourth that has five semi-tones, and there is an augmented fourth that has six semitones. The augmented fourth is exactly one half of the octave. There are no major or minor fifths either. There is a perfect fifth, having seven semitones, and a diminished fifth having six semitones. A diminished fifth sounds like an augmented fourth, but they are as different one from the other in their musical meaning as the word SOUL is from SOLE, even though both are pronounced the same.

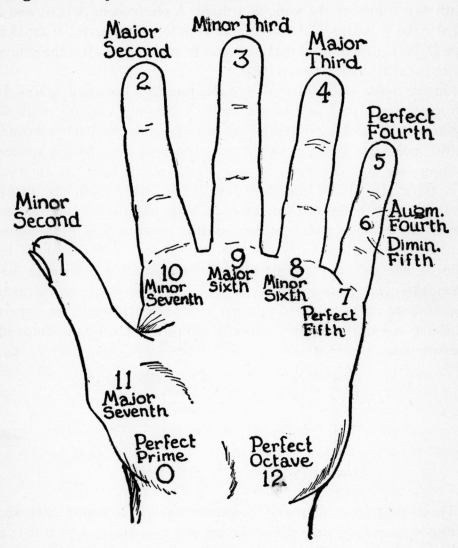

THE INTERVAL HAND

All these intervals, minor, major, augmented, diminished, and all these semitone numbers can be learned painlessly with the aid of the Interval Hand. Count 1, 2, 3, 4, 5, on the tips of the fingers of your left hand, from thumb to the little finger. Then count 6 in the middle joint of your little finger. Count 7 at the base of your little finger, and then count 8, 9, 10, and 11 on the bases of the rest of the fingers. Eight will come out at the base of the fourth finger, 9 at the base of the middle finger, and 10 at the base of the index finger. Eleven will come out at the base of the thumb. These numbers indicate semitones. Notice also that the numbers on the tip of each finger and at its base add up to 12. Keep this in mind for future reference. Now instead of counting 1 to 11 around your fingers, recite the following, while indicating the same places on your fingers as you did counting semitones:

> Minor Second
> Major Second
> Minor Third
> Major Third
> Perfect Fourth
> Augmented Fourth
> Perfect Fifth
> Minor Sixth
> Major Sixth
> Minor Seventh
> Major Seventh

Practice counting numbers from 1 to 11 around the left hand, and then intervals from the minor second to the major seventh until you are so certain of the numbers and the names that you can recite them backwards, counting from 11 to 1, from the major seventh to a minor second. Now try to find the right place for each interval at random. For instance, where is the interval of 5 semitones? Where is the minor third? Where is the augmented fourth? If you can answer these questions without hesitation, you ought to congratulate yourself on knowing the intervals and the number of semitones in each interval. How many semitones are there in a perfect fourth? (A perfect fourth is on the tip of your little finger.)

Now remember what we have said about the semitone numbers adding up to 12 on the tip and on the base of each finger. Notice that for each major interval on a fingertip there is a minor interval at its base, and vice versa. Recite your intervals in pairs; the one on the tip, and then the one at the base of each finger, like this: minor second, major seventh; major second, minor seventh; minor third, major sixth; major third, minor sixth; perfect fourth, perfect fifth. The augmented fourth and the diminished fifth are in the same place, in the middle joint of the little finger.

These opposite intervals are called inversions. Any interval and its inversion add up to an octave. For instance, a minor third has three semitones. The inversion of a minor third, according to our Interval Hand is a major sixth, and it has 9 semitones. Three plus 9 makes 12 semitones, and the interval having twelve semitones is an octave. Inversions are musical opposites, like black and white, small and large. Minor intervals are inversions of major intervals, and augmented intervals are inversions of diminished intervals. But a perfect interval remains perfect even when inverted. The inversion of a perfect fifth is a perfect fourth. The inversion of an octave is a unison, two notes on the same sound, or the same note played by two fingers. This zero interval is called a prime, or more completely, a perfect prime. The word prime means first, as in prime minister. On the Interval Hand we place the perfect prime opposite the perfect octave, on the wrist, seeing that fingertips and finger bases are already occupied.

Let us practice intervals from every single note on the piano, white or black. What is a minor third from F? Count three semitones. We reach A flat. But is it really A flat? Perhaps it is G sharp. After a moment's reflection, we decide in favor of A flat, because the interval is a third, and the third note from F is some kind of A.

Let us find a perfect fourth from F. A perfect fourth is situated on the tip of your little finger, and has five semitones. Counting five semitones from F we find B flat. This is the only perfect fourth from a white key that comes up to a black key. All other perfect fourths result in pairs of white keys, C to F, D to G, E to A.

Perfect fifths from white keys are also white notes, except one from B, which falls on F sharp. From black keys, perfect fourths come out on black keys, all except one. Which one? It is easy to find out. From F sharp a perfect fourth will come out on a white key, B. As for fifths, the only "black-white" one is from B flat to F.

When we tell time, we do not say, "It is now seven fifty-nine," but rather, "It is one minute of eight." When figuring out intervals larger than half an octave, we too, can say "a semitone of an octave," instead of a major seventh. In this way, instead of counting eleven semitones up, for a major seventh, we count one semitone down. The note a major seventh up from C is the same as a minor second down, which is B. Let us figure out a major sixth up from D. A major sixth is an octave minus a minor third. So we must take a minor third down from D, which is B. Now let us find a minor sixth up from G. Invert it. The result is a major third. A major third down from G is E flat, and it is the same note that we would find by laboriously counting a minor sixth up. In short, all we need to know are the numbers of semitones for the small intervals up to the tip of your little finger on the Interval Hand. For the big intervals we use inversions, and count the result down instead of up.

Applying this method, you ought to be able to figure out in a fraction of a second the right notes for any interval on the piano. You might outshine even professional musicians who calculate their intervals the hard way. A thorough knowledge of intervals is a great help for transposition, that is, playing a musical piece in a different key. For instance, Three Blind Mice played on the white keys begins like this: E, D, C. In the interval language, this is a major second down, and another major second down. Now let us transpose Three Blind Mice to begin on G. A major second down from G is F, and a major second down from F is E flat. The transposed melody will come out like this: G, F, E flat. Thus the Three Blind Mice coming down from G, will land on a black key—as any blind mouse unable to tell light from dark is liable to do.

❧3❧

Scales, or Tonal Ladders

A SCALE is a ladder. That is the original meaning of the word scale, from the Latin, as you can easily find out for yourself by looking it up in the dictionary. A musical scale is a ladder of sounds, only in a musical ladder the steps are not even. They are sometimes whole steps, and sometimes half steps. As we know, there are seven steps in every musical scale, arranged in alphabetical order. A scale runs from A to A, or from C to C, or from F to F, from any letter-note to its namesake an octave higher.

Two scales are now in use: the major scale and the minor scale. The major scale is a musical ladder which consists of two whole steps, one half step, three whole steps, and a half step. Minor scales consist of one whole step, one half step, two whole steps, one half step, and again one whole step. Minor scales are derived from corresponding major scales by starting on the sixth note of the major scale. Such minor scales are called relative minor scales. For instance, A minor is the relative minor scale of C major. The C major scale runs on the white keys from C to C, and the A minor scale runs on white keys from A to A. Another way of describing a relative minor scale is to say that it begins a minor third lower than the corresponding major scale.

As you play a minor scale, you feel that there is something lacking at the end of the octave run. It doesn't seem to flow as easily to its destination an octave higher as the major scale. This is because minor scales have no leading tone. What is a leading tone? It is a note that is a half step or a minor second below the keynote of the scale, and the keynote is of course the first note. For instance, in C major, the leading tone is B. It lies a half step below C, and leads to the keynote. In the A minor scale, the last note before the keynote is G, situated a whole step below A. It does not lead to the keynote with the same inevitability as a half step. To make minor scales more satisfying to the ear, this last note is raised. In A minor, it becomes G sharp instead of G natural. As a result of this change, the interval from F to the next note becomes an augmented second, F to G sharp. This augmented second has three semitones or one and a half steps. Because an augmented second is hard to sing, it is often smoothed down by raising F to F sharp.

We see now that there are three different minor scales; one that is derived directly from the relative major scale without any extra sharps; one in which the last note of the scale is raised in order to provide a leading tone; and one in which the note before that leading tone is raised a half step, in order to smooth down the awkward interval of one and a half steps. The first arrangement is called a *natural* minor scale, because it is derived naturally from the relative major scale. The second is called a harmonic minor scale, because in it the leading tone makes better harmony; the third is named a melodic minor scale because in it the awkward interval of one and a half steps is made more melodious by the raising of the note before the leading tone.

Now let us write down the intervals of the major scale and the three different minor scales. All these intervals will be some kind of seconds: minor seconds, major seconds, and in the case of the harmonic minor scale an augmented second.

Major Scale

Major second, major second, minor second, major second, major second, major second, minor second.

Natural Minor Scale

Major second, minor second, major second, major second, minor second, major second, and major second.

Harmonic Minor Scale

Major second, minor second, major second, major second, minor second, augmented second, and minor second.

Melodic Minor Scale

Major second, minor second, major second, major second, major second, major second, and minor second.

We know that the C major scale runs on white keys. Now we can prove it scientifically, by counting the major and minor seconds that make up the major scale. In major scales starting on any other note we have to use the black keys. Let us start a major scale on G, counting the intervals as we did in C major. We discover that we will have to use a black key, F sharp on the last note before the keynote. So G major has one sharp, namely F sharp, which is placed in the key signature, at the beginning of the music staff. This key signature serves as a reminder that all F's, high or low, shall be raised to F sharp.

Let us investigate this newcomer, the F sharp. When we ran a major scale from C to C there were no sharps. Then we began on G, which is a fifth higher, and got one sharp. That one sharp happens to be the leading tone. If we start a major scale a fifth higher than G, we will get another sharp, and that new sharp ought to be the leading tone of D major. In other words, every time we raise the keynote a fifth, we get a new sharp on the leading tone. In this way we can name the new sharp of any major scale. For instance, the new sharp of A major is its leading tone, that is, G sharp. The new sharp of E major is D sharp. The new sharp of B major is A sharp. But what is the new sharp of the F sharp major scale? Why, it is E sharp. Of course, it looks and sounds like F natural, but we must not forget that musical scales are ladders, that they have seven rungs, with a letter for every note of the musical alphabet. To write down key signatures properly, we must tabulate the sharps, according to the order of their appearances as leading tones: F sharp, C sharp, G sharp, D sharp, A sharp, E sharp. These sharps follow the cycle of fifths. C sharp is a fifth higher than F sharp; G sharp is a fifth higher than C sharp, and so on.

You can visualize the major scales and the new sharps by playing the keynotes on the piano beginning with the lowest C, and running upwards by fifths: C, G, D, A, E, and B. When you arrive at B, don't forget that a fifth from B is F sharp, and not F. F sharp is just about in the middle of the piano (the exact middle of the piano keyboard in case you are interested, is the crack between E and F, opposite the manufacturer's name). Continuing by fifths from F sharp, we will get scales with seven sharps and more. They are hardly ever used, but we might as well figure them out. C sharp major would have seven sharps, that is a sharp on every note. G sharp major ought to have eight sharps. But there are only seven notes in a scale, so one of the notes would have to be a double sharp. The scale with nine sharps will be D sharp major; a scale with ten sharps, A sharp major; with eleven sharps, E sharp major. A fifth above E sharp (which of course looks and sounds like F) is B sharp. Believe it or not, the B sharp major scale is played on the white keys. It sounds and looks like C major, but it has two sharps and five double sharps, which add up to twelve sharps. You might ask: Who in his right senses would write down all these double sharps, when the result is the same as no sharps at all? Well, Chopin did it once, in one of his Etudes.

THESE CHORDS (FROM CHOPIN'S ETUDE NO. 10, OP. 25) ARE ON WHITE KEYS, DESPITE THE SHARPS AND DOUBLE SHARPS

Now let us figure out scales with flats. All we need to do is reckon fifths down, starting from the highest C of the piano keyboard. A fifth below C is F, and F major has one flat. But which flat? Well, it is the middle note of the F scale that get flatted, and that is B. B flat is the first flat to appear in key signatures. Let us continue going down by fifths. A fifth below F is B flat, and the middle note between two B flats is E. This is the note that will get flatted. So B flat major has two flats. Going down by fifths we find that E flat major has three flats, A flat major has four flats, D flat major has five flats, G flat major has six flats, and C flat major has seven flats. In C flat major every note is flatted. We can go on into F flat major, which will have a double flat. The first flat to occur was B flat, and the first double flat will be B double flat. The scale with 9 flats will be B double flat major; the scale with 10 flats will be E double flat major. The scale with 11 flats will be A double flat major, and the scale with 12 flats, D double flat major. This time, you will not be surprised to find that D double flat major runs on the white keys. It is C major in disguise.

Here are some recipes for memorizing the number of sharps in major scales. The capital letter D is formed by two strokes, a line, and a curve, and D major has two sharps. The capital letter A has three strokes, and A major has three sharps. E has four strokes, and E major has four sharps. You can remember that F sharp major has six sharps by spelling out F Sharp, and counting the letters, F - S - H - A - R - P.

Major and minor scales are not the only ones that exist in music. It is quite possible to arrange thousands and thousands of new scales, and even split the semitone into smaller intervals. After all, the atom has been split, so why not split a semitone? A Mexican composer, Julian Carrillo, did exactly that. He split the musical atom into quarter-tones, eighth-tones, and sixteenth-tones, and invented scales of 24, 48, and 96 notes.

But even without splitting the semitone, we can make new scales by shuffling around the whole tones and semitones of the major scale. In fact, some of these scales, called Modes, are much more ancient than our major and minor scales. You can learn Modes by playing scales on white keys, beginning not only on C, but on D, on E, or on any other white key.

Play a scale from D to D, on white keys only. It will sound strange to our modern ears, but in old music, it was one of the most popular scales. It is called the Dorian Mode, a name which is easy to remember if you say, "D for Dorian, from D to D on white keys only." Incidentally, the Dorian Mode is reversible. When you play it downwards on white keys, from high D to D an octave lower, the intervals come out the same as when it is played upwards. The Dorian Mode is the only one that does this.

The Mode from E to E on white keys is named Phrygian. Note that it begins with a minor second, between E and F. The Mode played on white keys from F to F is the Lydian Mode. This Mode is the only one that has three whole steps in succession at the beginning, F, G, A, B. The next Mode, from G to G, is the Mixolydian. It sounds like a major scale without an F sharp. The Mode on A is the Aeolian. It is identical with the minor natural scale. You can remember the Aeolian Mode by saying, "A for Aeolian, from A to A, on white keys only." The Mode from B to B, called Locrian, is hardly ever used on account of the unpleasant diminished fifth between its first and fifth notes. Our major scale, too, is a Mode, and it has a name, the Ionian Mode, from C to C.

Play Modes as you would play ordinary major scales, and soon you will begin to enjoy their strange antiquated color. Play them from every note on the piano, on black keys as well as on white keys, by following the intervals of each Mode. An easy way to learn how to play Modes from any note, is to remember that the Dorian Mode begins on the second note of the major scale, the Phrygian on the third note, the Lydian on the fourth, the Mixolydian on the fifth, the Aeolian on the sixth, and the Locrian on the seventh. Suppose you want to play the Phrygian Mode beginning on F sharp. The Phrygian is the third Mode, and F sharp is the third note of D major. So all you have to do is to play the D major scale from F sharp to F sharp, and that will be the Phrygian Mode on F sharp.

Major and minor scales and the Modes have seven different notes each. But there are scales with only five or six notes. Five-note scales are called Pentatonic scales, from the word Penta, which means five in Greek. The Pentatonic scale is frequently called the black-key scale, because it can be played entirely on black keys, beginning either on F sharp or on E flat. The Chinese scale is pentatonic, and so are other Oriental scales. So if you like to compose music in the Oriental manner, play a melody on black keys, with an accompaniment in "black fifths," that is, E flat plus B flat, or G flat plus D flat, in the left hand. Composition in the pentatonic scale is foolproof, because any melody on black keys will agree with a black-key accompaniment.

A recent newcomer in the family of musical scales is the whole-tone scale which consists of whole steps only, C, D, E, F sharp, G sharp, B flat, C. There is no key signature, and the notes may be written either in sharps or in flats. There must be something sinister in the sound of the whole-tone scale because it is used on the radio and in the movies whenever there are spies, supernatural monsters, or mad scientists at work.

And then there is the chromatic scale, in semitones only. The word chromatic comes from chromos, which is *color* in Greek. The color is supplied by the sharps and flats. According to usage, a chromatic scale is written in sharps going up and flats coming down, but there are no absolutely set rules about that.

Among unusual scales which are neither major nor minor, there is the Gypsy scale, C, D, E flat, F sharp, G, A flat, B, and C. It has a certain ingratiating quality, and is very effective in rapid dancing tunes played on the violin.

You can make up any number of new scales for your own use, and here is the recipe. Divide the octave into two equal parts, from C to F sharp, and from F sharp to the next C. Insert two notes between C and F sharp, say E flat and F, and insert two notes between F sharp and the next C at the same intervals. You will obtain a six-note scale: C, E flat, F, F sharp, A, B, and C. Now insert three notes between C and F sharp, say D, E, F, and three notes between F sharp and the next C, using the same intervals. You will get this scale: C, D, E, F, F sharp, G sharp, A sharp, B, C. It is a double scale with four notes in C major and four notes in F sharp major.

An interesting scale can be made up by alternating whole tones and semitones. This is how it will come out: C, D, E flat, F, F sharp, G sharp, A, B, C. Play these newfangled scales on your piano and you will obtain an unusual modernistic effect.

4

How to Understand Rhythm

IN ORDER to learn musical scales we have to know the alphabet from A to G. In order to understand rhythm, we have to know how to add up fractions. Musical pieces are divided by bar lines into bars or measures. At the beginning of each musical piece, there is a time-signature that shows how many notes there are in a bar. 4/4 time is called common time because it is used more often than any other time signature. In 4/4 time there are four quarter-notes to a measure. This 4/4 time signature is like a dollar bill. You can change a dollar into four quarters, but you can also have a half a dollar and two quarters, so in 4/4 time you can have either four quarter-notes, or a half-note and two quarter-notes. And, of course, you can write down two half-notes, and that will make up a bar in 4/4 time. Or if you prefer musical silver dollars, you can write a whole note, which will take up the whole bar.

You know, of course, that a 25 cent piece is called two bits. A quarter-note can also be split into two bits, and each bit will be an eighth-note. Keep dividing these notes in two, and you will get 16th notes, 32nd notes, 64th notes, and 128th notes. There are even 256th notes, but they are a great rarity. In order to fill a bar in 4/4 time, you can use any combination of these fractions, provided they add up to four quarter-notes, or to one whole note.

A MUSICAL RARITY: 256TH NOTES (*Couperin*)

The same rule for adding fractions holds for any time signature. 3/4 time, or waltz time, can be filled in with three quarter-notes, or a half-note and a quarter-note, or three groups of two eighth-notes each.

A whole note is a white circle without a stem or a tail. A half-note is also a white circle, but it has a stem, and looks like a toy balloon on a stick. A quarter-note is a black circle with a stem. An eighth-note is a black circle with a flag attached to it. As we go into smaller fractions, we add more and more flags. A 16th note has two flags, a 32nd note has three flags, and a 64th note four flags. When there are several of these flagged notes in succession, they are joined together by parallel lines. A group of 16th notes is joined by two lines; 32nd notes by three lines; 256th notes would have six lines.

What if a musical note lasts three quarter-notes? In this case, we have to write a half-note and a quarter-note and put a tie over them to show that they are not two separate notes, but a single sound, three quarter-notes in duration. But there is a simpler way of making a three-quarter note: just put a dot after a half-note. This dot adds one-half to the value of the half-note, that is, a quarter-note. A sound that lasts three eighth-notes is represented by a quarter-note with a dot after it. A dotted eighth-note equals three sixteenth-notes. Figure out for yourself the value of a dotted 128th note.

Double dots and even triple dots are sometimes used. Every dot is worth one-half of the preceding dot. A double-dotted half-note equals one half-note, plus one quarter-note, plus one eighth-note, that is seven eighth-notes in all. A triple-dotted half-note equals fifteen 16th-notes, and a quadruply-dotted eighth-note equals thirty-one 128th notes. Such multiple dots rarely occur, so don't bother figuring them out unless you are especially fond of arithmetical calculations. To test your skill, fill up a 4/4 bar by using one each of the notes from a half-note down to a 128th note plus two 256th notes.

As you must have noticed, all these numbers are divisible by 2. But what if it is necessary to divide a quarter-note into three even notes? In such a case, you put the number 3 over three eighth-notes, indicating that there are three notes to one quarter-note, instead of the regular two. Such groups of three are called triplets. Groups of four are quadruplets; groups of five—well you have heard of the famous set of five Dionne girls. In music, too, five of a kind are called quintuplets.

Sixteenth Notes

Eighth Notes

Dotted Eighth Notes

Quarter Notes

Dotted Quarter Notes

Half Note

Dotted Half Note

NOTE DURATIONS IN RHYTHM CAGES

In the orchestral piece, *Pacific 231,* its composer, Arthur Honegger, describes in musical tones a giant American locomotive. The engine starts off making two puffs to a bar in 4/4 time, then three puffs, then four, and five. To indicate the number of puffs, there are figures over each group of notes, three half-notes marked 3, or five quarter-notes marked 5.

In order to familiarize yourself with musical fractions that make up the language of rhythm, do this: cut out a couple of dozen strips of heavy paper about six inches in length each. Cut some of them in two, some in three pieces, others in four, six, and twelve pieces. Write a dotted half-note on each 6-inch strip; dotted quarter-notes on 3-inch strips; quarter-notes on 2-inch strips; dotted eighth-notes on 1½-inch strips, eighth-notes on 1-inch strips; and sixteenth-notes on half-inch strips. Mark the time signature of 4/4 and fill in each bar with different notes. After a dotted half-note use a quarter-note. After a dotted quarter-note, use an eighth-note; after a dotted eighth-note, use a sixteenth-note. Generally speaking a dotted note ought to be followed by a note one-third its value.

4/4, 3/4, and 2/4 time signatures are the most common in music. Among time signatures in eighth-notes, the numerator is usually a multiple of 3, as 3/8, 6/8, 9/8 and 12/8. Occasionally we find time signatures in sixteenth-notes, as for instance, 3/16 and 6/16. Although in arithmetic 6/8 is the same as 3/4, in music they are different. 3/4 time has three beats, while 6/8 time has two beats; 3/4 time and 6/8 time are as different as a waltz and a jig.

Whatever time signature is indicated in a musical piece, the denominator is never an odd number. There are no such time signatures as 2/3, 6/7, or 6/9, because there are no third-notes, seventh-notes, or ninth-notes.

Rhythm is the spice of music. It enlivens the simplest scale. Play a scale up and down in this rhythm: half-note, quarter-note, two eighth-notes, and again half-note, quarter-note, two eighth-notes. You will be amazed what fine melodies will result from it. Rhythmic arpeggios (that is, broken chords) are also very effective. By skillful combination of scales and arpeggios in a definite rhythmic pattern, you can recreate the great themes of classical music. And no wonder: scales, arpeggios, and rhythm are the principal ingredients of melody.

THESE RHYTHMS UNDERLIE MANY GREAT MELODIES

Silence in music is as important as the actual notes. It is indicated by special signs appropriately called rests. A whole-note rest is a black rectangle below a line; a half-note rest is a similar rectangle placed above a line. A quarter-note rest is a vertical wiggle. An eighth-note rest looks like the figure 7. For 16th-note rests, 32nd-note rests, etc., you add extra flags to the 7-like eighth-note rest. These rests may be dotted, too, in which case they become fifty percent longer.

Not all musicians appreciate the importance of musical silence. When a piano student was told to learn the second movement of a

Beethoven Sonata which has many long rests, he complained to the teacher that he could not very well afford to pay the full price for his lessons if he had to waste half the time just waiting between the notes!

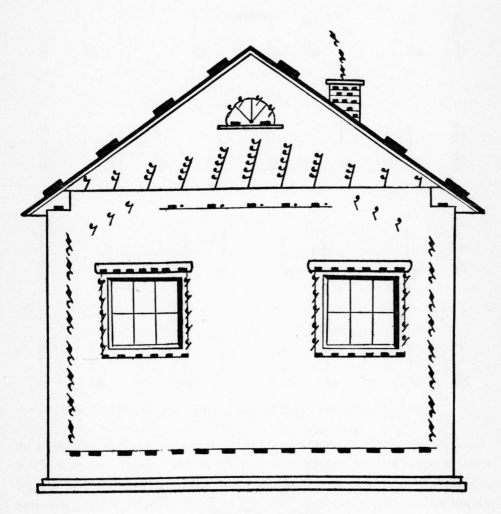

A REST-FUL HOUSE

What Is Harmony?

HARMONY means many things to many people. We speak of harmony in human relations and of international harmony. The ancients believed in a celestial harmony of the sun, the moon, and the planets revolving in a crystal sphere in the firmament. On starry nights they thought one could hear this harmony of the spheres, inexpressibly beautiful and inspiring.

In music, harmony is the science of arranging chords in a manner that is pleasing to the ear. By tradition, these chords are arranged in thirds. A chord of three notes, like C, E, and G, is called a triad, meaning a threesome. A chord of four different notes like G, B, D, F, is a seventh chord.

As we know, there are two kinds of thirds, major thirds and minor thirds. A triad that is made up of a major third between the bottom note and the middle note, and a minor third between the middle note and the top, is called a major triad. A minor triad is a major triad turned upside down. In it, a minor third is at the bottom, and a major third is on top. A triad composed of two minor thirds is called a diminished triad. Why? Because two minor thirds add up to a diminished fifth, and so the triad itself is called a diminished triad. Triads made up of two major thirds are called augmented triads. In this case the interval from bottom to top is an augmented fifth.

Triads can be built in a simple way, by skipping every other note in the musical alphabet. Let us write out a musical alphabet from A to G twice over.

A B C D E F G A B C D E F G

Pick out any letter-note at will, say E, then skip every other note. The triad on E will be E, G, B. This is a minor triad, because from E to G is a minor third, and from G to B is a major third. Now let us pick a triad on B. It will come out B, D, F. This is a diminished triad because both thirds are minor thirds, and the interval from bottom to top is a diminished fifth. Practice on these triads until you can name them unfailingly, and quickly, too.

Here is a limerick, which ought to help in memorizing triads.

Let's sit at the piano and try it:

What makes $\dfrac{\text{a diminished}}{\text{an augmented}}$ triad?

Two $\dfrac{\text{minor}}{\text{major}}$ thirds together,

Two thirds of a feather

Will make the $\dfrac{\text{diminished}}{\text{augmented}}$ triad!

Read the upper of the double adjectives for the diminished triad, and the lower for the augmented triad.

We are familiar with inversions of intervals. An inverted third is a sixth, and an inverted sixth is a third. An inverted fourth is a fifth, and a fifth inverted becomes a fourth. When we invert an interval, we transfer the lower note of the interval an octave higher. To invert a chord, we do exactly the same. When we invert a triad, we take the bottom note and put it an octave higher, without changing the rest of the chord. This way we get a chord consisting of a third and a fourth, adding up to a sixth. It may sound strange that a third plus a fourth should be a sixth, while 3 plus 4 equals 7. This unusual arithmetic comes from the fact that we are adding alphabet distances rather than numbers. From A to C is a third, and from C to F is a fourth. The sum of these two intervals is A to F which is a sixth.

The names of chords are usually counted by the intervals from the bottom. The inversion of a triad is called a 6/3 chord. Let us invert this 6/3 chord. Again we take the bottom note and put it an octave higher. Now we get a fourth on the bottom, and a third on the top. A fourth plus a third makes a sixth according to our alphabetical arithmetic. So the second inversion of a triad is a 6/4 chord, as we count the intervals from the bottom to the top and from the bottom to the middle note.

To make inversions of chords absolutely clear, I recommend the following game. Get hold of some heavy construction paper, black or any dark hue, and cut out a crescent, a heart, and a triangle—each about the size of the width of a white key on the piano. Put the heart on the middle C, the crescent on E, and the triangle on G. This will be the C major triad. Now take the heart from the middle C and put it on the C an octave above. This will make a 6/3 chord. You can count these intervals from the bottom note, a sixth from E to C, and a third from E to G. Then invert the 6/3 chord by placing the crescent on E an octave higher. The result will be a 6/4 chord, which is the second inversion of the triad. Invert it once more by transferring the triangle from G to the G an octave higher, and you will get your triad back again.

If you have memorized your Interval Hand to the last knuckle, you will know exactly what kinds of thirds, fourths, and sixths you will be getting as you invert major, minor, or diminished triads. In the first inversion of a major triad, you will find a minor third from the bottom to the middle note, and a minor sixth from the bottom to the top note. Inverting a minor triad, you will find that its 6/3 chord has a major third and a major sixth. If you are confused by the fact that in the first inversion of a major triad, the intervals are minor, just remember that inversions invert, that is, they turn your intervals upside down and

A TRIAD. THE HEART IS THE ROOT OF THE CHORD

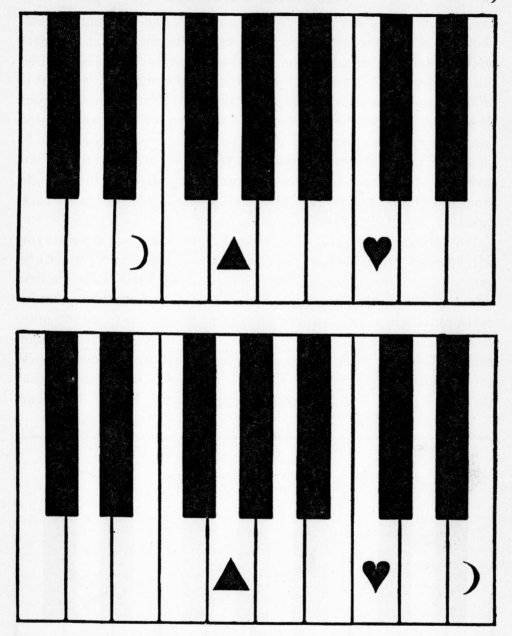

INVERSIONS OF A TRIAD. THE HEART IS THE ROOT OF
THE CHORD

inside out. Major becomes minor, and minor becomes major. Practice
your triads and inversions on every white key and then try black ones.
Now that you know the exact intervals in major and minor triads

and their inversions, try to build these chords on a single note. For instance, a major triad on C is C, E, G. The major 6/3 chord on C is C, E flat, and A flat (remember that in a major 6/3 chord, the intervals are minor, and counted from C will come out on black keys). The major 6/4 chord from C is C, F, A.

Now let us take up the minor chords. A minor triad on C is C, E flat, G; a minor 6/3 chord (which, you must not forget, has major intervals) will be C, E, and A; and a minor 6/4 chord will be C, F, and A flat. Play all these chords very slowly one after another. The change of harmonies will produce a pleasing ethereal effect.

Musical Shorthand

SHORTHAND is not a new invention. It was known in ancient Rome, and it was by shorthand that the speeches of great Roman orators have been preserved. In America, no business office can carry on without a secretary proficient in the art of putting the mumbled words and phrases of a nervous executive into little lines and curves that are magically transformed into typewritten sentences.

There is shorthand in music, too. It is infinitely simpler than secretarial shorthand, for it is made up only of Roman and Arabic numerals, which indicate intervals, counted from the bass up. They are adequate for an analysis of classical compositions, but in modern music, shorthand may turn out to be as complicated as this: "The pusillanimity of the secessionists jeopardizes the doctrine of extraterritoriality."

Musical shorthand is called Figured Bass. The figures under the bass note correspond to the interval from that note upwards. For instance, in Figured Bass, a triad is 5/3, to show that the upper note is a fifth from the bass, and the middle note is a third from the bass. Octaves are not marked, for they are simply duplications. Traditional harmony is in four parts, and for this reason, one note has to be doubled when triads or their inversions are used. For instance, the C major triad arranged in four-part harmony will have two C's, like this: C, E, G, C. The three upper notes may be shuffled at will, and still the chord will remain C major. Thus, C major chords can be arranged in six different ways:

C E G C
C E C G
C G C E
C G E C
C C E G
C C G E

In four-part harmony, the notes in a chord are named after human voices, Bass, Tenor, Alto, and Soprano. The word Soprano means highest in Italian. It carries the melody. But the chords are named not after the Soprano, but after the Bass. The Bass is the boss. It gives each chord its name. As for the Tenor and the Alto, they are the least important. They serve merely to fill in the harmony.

THE BASS IS THE BOSS. IT GIVES EACH CHORD ITS NAME

Arabic numbers are used to indicate the intervals from the Bass up. Roman numerals show the degrees of the scale. There are seven degrees in each scale, and they bear special names, Tonic, Supertonic, Mediant, Subdominant, Dominant, Submediant, and Leading Tone. Perhaps we ought to explain the origin of some of these names. The Leading Tone leads to the Tonic and is sometimes called the Subtonic. The Supertonic is above the Tonic. The Mediant is in the middle between the Tonic and the Dominant. The Subdominant is under the Dominant, as subway is under the way. The Submediant is a secondary Mediant, in the sense that a subdivision is a secondary division. As to the Dominant, it dominates the dominion of the predominating domain among chords, and so is called the Dominant. At least this is the only reasonable explanation, for in all candor the Tonic is the dominating chord in harmony, and not the Dominant.

C, E, G is a tonic triad in C major, and it is expressed in musical shorthand by the symbol I_3^5, or simply I. By tradition, Roman numerals without the small Arabic numbers denote triads in root position, that is triads arranged in thirds, with the root of the triad in the Bass. In 6/3 chords, the root is a sixth above the Bass, and in 6/4 chords, it is a fourth above the Bass.

What is the chord D, F, B in the key of C major? D is the bass. From D to B above is a sixth, and from D up to F is a third. The chord is therefore a 6/3 chord. We know that in a 6/3 chord, the root is on top, but we can make sure of it by reinverting the chord and placing the top note an octave lower, B, D, F. This is the Leading Tone triad. We have now found that the root is the Leading Tone, marked as the Roman numeral VII. The name of the chord is therefore VII_3^6.

Now let us determine the musical shorthand symbol for the chord B, E, G, assuming that we are in C major. It is a six-four chord, and its root is in the middle. In C major, the note E is the Mediant, and it is marked by the Roman numeral III. Therefore, B, E, G is III_4^6. Now let us figure out A, C, F. Counting the intervals, we find that this is a six-three chord, and in six-three chords, the root is on top. Again assuming that we are in C major, F is the Subdominant, and the chord is IV_3^6. The same chord in F major would be the Tonic 6/3 chord. In B flat major, it would be the Dominant 6/3 chord, and in D minor, the Mediant 6/3. These changing chords are very important in Modulation, which will be discussed in a later chapter.

∽7∾

Fitting Chords to Melody

IN HARMONY, the most important chords are the Tonic triad, the Sub-dominant triad, and the Dominant triad. In C major the Tonic triad is C, E, G; the Subdominant triad is F, A, C; and the Dominant triad is G, B, D. If we write all these letters in alphabetical order, we will get every note of the C major scale, C, D, E, F, G, A, B, C. Let us now take a minor scale. The Tonic, the Subdominant, and the Dominant in A minor will be A, C, E; D, F, A; and E, G, B. Let us arrange these letter-notes in alphabetical order: A, B, C, D, E, F, G, A. This musical alphabet spells the entire A minor scale. Thus we find that the Tonic, the Subdominant, and the Dominant triads together in-clude every note of the scale. Furthermore, in major keys, these three triads are major, and in minor they are minor. The only exception is the minor harmonic scale, in which the Dominant is a major triad.

> The Tonic, Subdominant, Dominant
> In every key are most prominent;
> In major they're major,
> In minor they're minor,
> But the minor harmonic has a major Dominant

Because these three triads take in every note of the scale, we can harmonize any melody with their aid. If we make a computation of chords in a classical sonata or a symphony, we will find that the Tonic, Subdominant, and Dominant triads occur more often than other chords. The Supertonic triad and the Mediant triad are used but rarely, and the Leading Tone triad, practically never, because it is a diminished triad, and is awkward to handle. Among 6/3 chords, the Tonic 6/3 chord and Supertonic 6/3 chord are used more often than other 6/3 chords. Among 6/4 chords, the Tonic 6/4 chord is prac-tically the only one that occurs in simple music. Let us tabulate the most popular harmony chords.

A HARMONY LIMERICK

Chords Most Often Used in Harmony

Triads	I	IV	V
6/3 Chords	I_3^6	II_3^6	
6/4 Chords	I_4^6		

Learn these chords in every key, and try to recognize them quickly when they occur in classical music. With the aid of these chords you will be able to produce a fairly competent harmonization of melodies in the classical style.

Among seventh chords, the most important is the Dominant Seventh. It is made up of two major thirds and one minor third. It is the same as a major triad with a minor third on top. This will give you an easy recipe for constructing a Dominant Seventh chord on any note, even without knowing in what key you are. For instance, a Dominant Seventh chord on C is a major triad, C, E, G, and a minor third on top of it, that is B flat. And seeing that it is the Dominant Seventh, C must be the Dominant, and the Tonic is F. So we are in the key of F, either major or minor.

When a seventh-chord is inverted, the Bass goes over the top, and is placed an octave higher. In the Dominant Seventh chord G, B, D, F, the root is always G, marked with the Roman numeral V. The intervals are indicated in Arabic numbers counting from the Bass up, because the Bass is the Boss. The shorthand symbol for a Dominant Seventh chord is V_7. Its first inversion is $V{}^6_5$, the second inversion $V{}^6_{43}$, and the third inversion $V{}^6_{42}$.

```
                            1 2 3 4 5 6 7
                          1 2 3 4 5 6 7 1
                        1 2 3 4 5 6 7 1 2
                      1 2 3 4 5 6 7 1 2 3
                    1 2 3 4 5 6 7 1 2 3 4
                  1 2 3 4 5 6 7 1 2 3 4 5
                1 2 3 4 5 6 7 1 2 3 4 5 6
              1 2 3 4 5 6 7 1 2 3 4 5 6 7
            1 2 3 4 5 6 7 1 2 3 4 5 6 7 1
          1 2 3 4 5 6 7 1 2 3 4 5 6 7 1 2
        1 2 3 4 5 6 7 1 2 3 4 5 6 7 1 2 3
      1 2 3 4 5 6 7 1 2 3 4 5 6 7 1 2 3 4
    1 2 3 4 5 6 7 1 2 3 4 5 6 7 1 2 3 4 5
  1 2 3 4 5 6 7 1 2 3 4 5 6 7 1 2 3 4 5 6
1 2 3 4 5 6 7 1 2 3 4 5 6 7 1 2 3 4 5 6 7
A B C D E F G A B C D E F G A B C D E F G
```

With the aid of this table, you can name any chord at once. The numbers indicate intervals from a prime to a seventh. Suppose we have a chord F, D, B, G. Locate the row which has number 1 over F. Now find the numbers in the same row which are over D, B, and G. Any D, B, and G will do, because as we know, the name of the chord remains the same, no matter what the order of the three upper notes. When you look up these numbers, you find 6 over D, 4 over B, and 2 over G. So the chord must be a six-four-two chord. In order to find the root of this chord, we must invert it to its original position as a seventh chord, G, B, D, F. The root is G, which is the Dominant in C major, so the name of the chord is V_2^6.

As a matter of fact, it is not necessary to invert a chord to its original position in order to find the root. If a chord is an inversion of a seventh chord, the root will be the second of two neighboring notes, like F and G. Using this recipe, let us find the root of the chord C, G, E, A. The two neighboring letter-notes are G and A, so A is the root, and the complete name of the chord, assuming we are still in C major, is VI_3^6. Check on this by the table. Now figure out the following chord: D, F, C, A. It is II_7. What is the symbol for the chord B, E, G, D? The two neighboring notes are D and E, so E is the root. The name of the chord is III_4^6. Now figure out the chord D, B, F, A. It is VII_3^6. Check it by the table.

Now let us learn how to connect chords in four-part harmony. The most important law is to lead each voice to the nearest available note of the next chord, the Law of the Nearest Way. If there are common tones in two successive chords, such common tones should be kept in the same voice. Suppose we connect the Tonic triad with the Dominant triad. The C major triad and the Dominant triad both have G, so the voice that has the G will not move. The voice that has E will move to D, which is the nearest note to it in the Dominant chord. The Bass will of course move to G, because the Bass is the boss, and it can jump or move gradually according to plan. There is still another C in the C major chord in four-part harmony. That C will move to B.

Let us connect the C major triad with the Dominant six-four-three chord. The Bass of the Dominant six-four-three chord will be D, and the rest of the notes will be F, G, and B. Let us compare these notes with the C major triad. The Bass will move from C to D; the common tone G will remain where it is. E will move to F, and the extra C in the C major chord will move to B.

When the three upper voices are bunched together within a space less than an octave, the chords are in Close Harmony. When the three upper voices are spread over more than an octave, the chords are in Open Harmony. But the distance between the Soprano and Alto, or the Alto and Tenor should not be over an octave. It is all right, however, to have more than an octave between the Bass and the Tenor.

When in doubt, the best rule is to move the three upper voices in contrary motion to the Bass. When the Bass moves up, it is good to move at least two of the upper voices down. When the Bass moves down, some of the upper voices should go up. This rule is particularly important when there is no common tone. For instance, when we connect the Subdominant triad with the Dominant triad, the Bass goes one step up, and the three upper voices should all go down.

Among traditional rules of harmony is the prohibition of consecutive octaves and consecutive fifths. If one of the voices moves, let us say from C to D, no other voice should move from C to D, or else there will be consecutive octaves, which sound monotonous. Moreover, in this example, a G should not go to A, because C with G will make up a fifth, and D with A will make up another fifth.

> Consecutive octaves or fifths in good harmony
> Ought not to be used lest ears they might harm any.
> 　　If F goes to G,
> 　　Don't move C to D,
> Or else these bad fifths will result in disharmony.

8

The Modulation Clock

EVERY piece of music must end in the key in which it has started—at least that is the accepted convention. But between the beginning and the end there is a great deal of going to and fro through different keys. Going from one key to another is called Modulation.

We may not realize it, but as a matter of fact, every key includes six tonalities. The Supertonic triad in C major is D, F, and A, and it is at the same time the Tonic triad of D minor. The Mediant triad in C major is E, G, and B, and it is at the same time the Tonic triad of E minor. The Subdominant triad of C major is F, A, and C, and it is at the same time the Tonic triad of F major. The Dominant triad in C major is G, B, D, and it is at the same time the Tonic triad of G major. The Submediant triad in C major is A, C, and E, and it is at the same time the Tonic triad of A minor. The Leading-Tone triad, B, D, F, isn't anything, because it is a diminished triad, and there is no such thing as a diminished key.

It follows then that we can modulate from C major into D minor, E minor, F major, G major, or A minor, by just playing the Supertonic, Mediant, Subdominant, Dominant, or Submediant triad, and then regard the modulation as completed. For instance, in C major, we play the Mediant triad, E, G, B, and then say: "This is no longer the Mediant of C major, but the Tonic triad of E minor."

Notice that all these keys that are present in C major have either one flat or one sharp in the key signature, or no flats, no sharps. D minor has one flat; E minor has one sharp; F major has one flat, G major has one sharp, A minor has no sharps, no flats. So from C major, which is a no-flat, no-sharp key, we can instantly modulate into any key which has either one sharp or one flat, and also into the relative minor key, which has no flats, no sharps.

Let us now take the key of D flat major, which has five flats, and see

what modulations are available from it. The Supertonic triad of D
flat major is E flat minor, which has six flats; the Mediant triad, F
minor has four flats (incidentally, a good way to memorize the key
signature of F minor is to say: F-f-f-f minor has f-f-f-four f-f-f-
flats); the Subdominant triad, G flat major, has six flats; the Dominant triad, A flat major has four flats, and the Submediant triad B
flat minor, has five flats. From this we conclude that a key in five flats
can modulate instantly into any key which has one flat more or one
flat less. You can easily guess that from E major, which has four sharps,
you can modulate into any key with three or five sharps. From F
major, which has one flat, you can modulate into a key with no flats,
or into a key with two flats. In other words, you can modulate into any
key that has one flat or sharp less, or one flat or sharp more than the key
you have started from.

Now let us consider the chords on the different degrees of a minor
key. Let us take A minor, which has no flats, no sharps. The Supertonic triad in A minor is B, D, F, which is a diminished triad. The
Mediant triad in A minor is C, E, G, and it is also the Tonic triad of
C major. The Subdominant of A minor is D, F, A, which is the Tonic
triad of D minor; the Dominant triad in the natural A minor scale is
E, G, B, which is the Tonic triad of E minor. The Submediant triad in
A minor is F, A, C, which is the Tonic triad of F major. The seventh
degree of the natural scale in A minor will give us G, B, D, which
is the Tonic triad of G major. Each of these triads have either one
sharp or one flat, so we can instantly modulate into any neighboring
key, by taking the desired chord and saying: "This is no longer the
Mediant (or whatever chord you choose), but the Tonic of a new
key."

In the minor harmonic scale, the Dominant is E, G sharp, and B.
At the same time, it is the Tonic of E major, which has four sharps. So
by taking the major dominant of a minor scale, we can modulate four
sharps ahead. From D minor, which has one flat, we can jump to its
Dominant, A major, which has three sharps. To do this, we must
add four sharps to one flat. But how can we add sharps to flats? Very
simple: sharps are positives, and flats negatives, and each sharp can-
cels a flat. So a key with one flat plus four sharps equals a key with
three sharps.

Let us modulate from G minor to D major. G minor has two flats. We add four sharps. Two flats neutralize two sharps, and two sharps are left over. As a result, we find ourselves modulated to a major key in two sharps, which is D major.

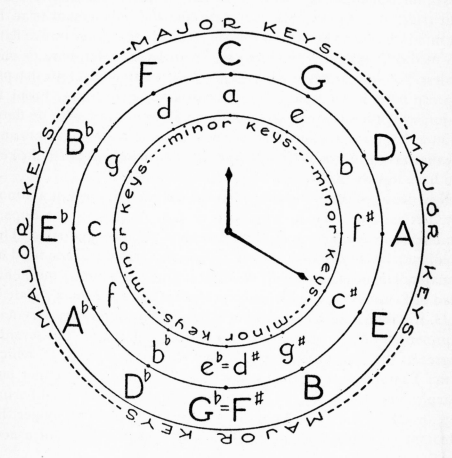

THE MODULATION CLOCK

We can also modulate four keys in reverse, from major to minor. For instance, C major is the major Dominant of F minor harmonic scale, and F-f-f-f minor has f-f-f-four f-f-f-flats. From G major we can modulate to C minor, because G major is the Dominant of C minor. In this case, one sharp in the key signature of G major is cancelled by one of the flats, and three flats remain in the key signature.

There are 12 major and 12 minor keys. And there are 12 hours on the face of a clock. By comparing keys to hours, we can construct a

Modulation Clock, which will show us as clearly as the time of day, how to go from one key to another. Let us call 12:00 the Zero Key. C major and A minor will show Zero hour, because C major and A minor have no sharps and no flats. G major and E minor will be at 1:00 o'clock, because they have one sharp in the key signature. D major will be at 2:00 o'clock; A major at 3:00 o'clock; E major at 4:00 o'clock; B major at 5:00 o'clock; F sharp major at 6:00 o'clock. Now let us consider the flat keys: 11:00 o'clock is one hour before Zero hour, and so it will show one flat in the key signature; 10:00 o'clock will have two flats; 9:00 o'clock will have three flats; 8:00 o'clock will have four flats; 7:00 o'clock will have five flats.

Six o'clock will be a key of six sharps or six flats. If we count from the sharp end, we will have F sharp major or D sharp minor; reckoning from the flat direction, 6:00 o'clock will be G flat major or E flat minor. So 6:00 o'clock is the demarcation line between the flats and the sharps, and we cannot cross it by modulation without renaming the keys.

Now let us modulate from any key to any other key on the face of the Modulation Clock. We can use either one-hour steps to the neighboring key, or four-hour jumps from minor to major, forwards, or four hours from major to minor, backwards. Suppose we want to modulate from C major to A major. C major is 12:00 o'clock, or Zero hour. The key of A major is at 3:00 o'clock. Instead of going hour by hour, we can go back one hour to a minor key, and then four hours forward to a major key, and we will land at 3:00 o'clock. This means going from C major to D minor (which is the Supertonic triad of C major), and from D minor to A major (which is the major Dominant of D minor). Now let us attempt a six-hour modulation from C major to F sharp major. We can make it in two one-hour jumps, and one four-hour jump. Let us go from C major to E minor, which is the Mediant of C major, and has one sharp in the key signature. From E minor we can jump to its major Dominant, which is B major, and from there it is next door to F sharp major. Let us write down the chords in this modulation: C major, E minor, B major, F sharp major, and let us draw a little clock above each chord, indicating the hour of each key according to its key signature. This will connect up chords, keys and clocks in our mind.

MODULATION BY THE CLOCK

Here are a few modulations to try on the Modulation Clock:

1. Modulate from B flat major to E major (hint: go via D minor)
2. Modulate from E minor to F minor (hint: go via C major)
3. Modulate from G flat major to C major (go first to B flat minor)
4. Modulate from A minor to B flat major (go hour by hour)
5. Modulate from D flat major to G sharp minor (go around the clock)

In order to smooth down modulations, transition chords are used between the triads. A very good chord to use between the Mediant and the Tonic, is the Dominant six-four-three chord. Suppose we modulate from C major to A minor. C major is the Mediant of A minor. So we use the Dominant six-four-three chord. One of the voices will progress chromatically, from G to G sharp (which is the leading tone in A minor) and into A, the keynote of A minor.

Now let us modulate from A minor to F major. Again A minor is the Mediant, and again we use the same $V^6_4{}_3$ chord, in the key to which we are going. From F major, using the same transition chord, we can modulate to D minor, from D minor to B flat major, and so on. In such a modulating chain, the Bass will keep moving down in the C major scale, then shifting to the B flat major scale. Try it over on your piano.

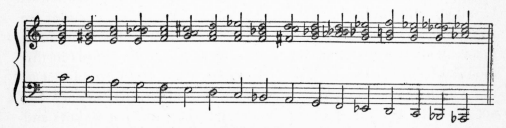

A CHAIN OF MODULATIONS

At the end of the modulation, we must have some sort of a concluding musical phrase, like a signature in a letter. There are formal signatures like, "Very truly yours," and there are the more florid ones, used in French correspondence, such as, "I beg you to agree to receive, my dear Sir, the expression of my very distinguished sentiments and the assurance of profoundest esteem."

A simple musical signature consists of the principal triads, the Tonic, Subdominant, Dominant, and once more the Tonic. Sometimes, the tonic six-four chord is added between the Subdominant and the Dominant. Such musical signatures are called Cadences.

As we know, the Bass is the boss. The Bass of the last chord in a musical piece is the key in which a composition is written. But sometimes a musical piece in a minor key ends in major. For instance, the *C Minor Fugue* of Bach ends on the C major chord. This is a time-honored device, which, for some reason, is known as the Third of Picardy, a major third, instead of minor.

You can easily spot a modulation by the appearance of new sharps or flats. Suppose a piece is written in C major, and after a few bars F sharp bobs up here and there rather persistently. That means that F sharp is the leading tone of a new key, so the persistent appearance of F sharp in a piece written in C major indicates a modulation into G major, because F sharp is the leading tone of the G major scale.

The rules of the Modulation Clock apply to modulations by means of triads. But there is a way of modulating instantly by using a special chord, a sort of musical chameleon, that changes its color according to circumstances. It is the Diminished Seventh chord. When inverted it will still have the same intervals of three semitones between each pair of voices. These intervals will be either augmented seconds or minor thirds. The augmented second is the inversion of a diminished seventh. And the diminished seventh itself sounds like a major sixth, but is spelled differently.

Let us arrange a Diminished Seventh chord in open harmony, like this: F sharp in the Bass, E flat in the Tenor, C in the Alto, and A in the Soprano. Suppose we want to modulate to C major. The notes of a C major chord are C, E, and G. The Bass will move from F sharp to G; the Tenor will move from E flat to E; the Alto will remain on C; and the Soprano will move from A to G. As a result, we will get the Tonic 6/4 chord in C major. And we know that the Tonic 6/4 chord is a part of the musical signature, the cadence. So all we have to do is to add a few concluding chords, and the modulation will be completed.

If we modulate from the same Diminished Seventh chord to D flat major, we will land on the tonic 6/3 chord. If we modulate into F sharp major, the Bass will remain on F sharp. Some of these progressions may sound rather strange, and this strangeness gives a unique color to this chord. That is why the Diminished Seventh chord is so often used in grand opera whenever dramatic effect is intended. The orchestra strikes the Diminished Seventh chord fortissimo, and the listener cannot tell what will happen next. This creates a feeling of dramatic suspense.

An unexpected example of the use of the Diminished Seventh chord is the story of a musical British flier who flew reconnaissance missions over the German lines during the African campaign. He radioed to the headquarters, whistling four notes, C, E flat, F sharp, A, repeating the message over and over again. Headquarters was puzzled, until a musically inclined officer volunteered the suggestion that the flier apparently tried to convey the intelligence that the seventh German division was diminished. He did so by whistling a Diminished Seventh chord.

Counterpoint, a Big Word Easily Explained

THERE are words that look impressive: Prerogative, Corollary, Conductivity. In music, the most impressive word is Counterpoint. Yet there is nothing mysterious about the meaning of this word. Counterpoint means Point Counter Point, and point in this case is a musical note.

1. Point is a Note.
2. Counter means Against.
3. Point is a Note.

Result: Point Counter Point means Note Against Note.

It follows then that Counterpoint is a science that teaches how to play or sing a note against another note. Of course, harmony teaches that, too, but in harmony the important thing is the proper connection of chords. In harmony, voices go to the nearest place, while in Counterpoint they move about with great independence. Harmony is set in four parts, but Counterpoint may be written in two parts, or three parts, or four parts, or more.

Most piano pieces are composed according to the rules of harmony, while compositions for several instruments, that is, chamber music works, follow the democratic ways of Counterpoint so as to allow individual voices to be heard.

In Counterpoint, as well as in harmony, chords are named by the intervals reckoned from the bass up. When we consider chords, it is harmony; when we follow the separate voices individually, it is Counterpoint. It is like an expertly woven fabric: when you look at the design as a whole, it is harmonic appreciation; when you follow the threads of individual colors, it is counterpoint.

If the separate voices are active and carry their own melodies, then there is more Counterpoint than harmony. If the individual parts do not move much, there is more harmony than Counterpoint. Contra-

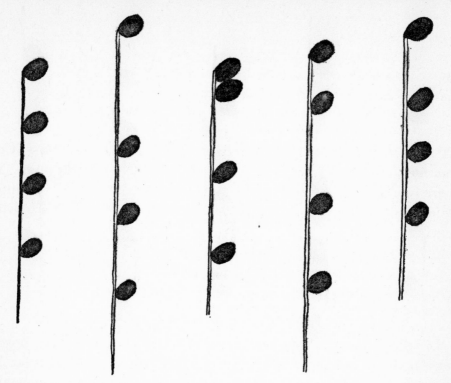

THIS IS HARMONY. THE VOICES COMBINE IN VERTICAL CHORDS

puntal voices are horizontal, moving from left to right. Harmony is vertical, forming perpendicular combinations or chords.

Although Counterpoint means a note against a note, there can also be points counter point, several notes against one note.

One note against one note is Counterpoint of the First Species.
Two notes against one note is Counterpoint of the Second Species.
Three, four, or any larger number of notes againt one note is Counterpoint of the Third Species.

The Fourth Species of Counterpoint is Syncopated Counterpoint. That means that the notes of the contrapuntal voices do not come together; they are out of step. The Fifth Species of Counterpoint is marked by free rhythm, syncopation, and ornamental melodic patterns.

It is easy to remember the First and the Second Species. The First Species has one note against one note. The Second Species has two notes against one. The Third Species includes not only three notes

THIS IS COUNTERPOINT. EACH VOICE MOVES HORIZONTALLY
ALONG ITS INDEPENDENT PATH

COUNTERPOINT OF THE SECOND SPECIES

against one, but also four notes, six notes, or eight notes against one. These notes must be even, all quarter-notes or all eighth-notes. If the notes are different, then it is free Counterpoint, in the Fifth Species.

Ask a friend, preferably a six-footer, to walk very slowly, making long strides. Walk alongside him making two steps to his one. That will be Counterpoint of the Second Species. Then walk four steps to his one stride. That will be Counterpoint of the Third Species. To demonstrate syncopated Counterpoint, you will have to team up with a fellow of your own size. Let him start walking rather slowly. After he has raised his foot, walk alongside, but out of step. That will be the Fourth Species or Syncopated Counterpoint. To illustrate the Fifth Species, make two slow steps and then two fast steps, then march out of step, then walk any way you like. But all this must be done in a rhythmic fashion, to create an impression of vigorous motion.

SYNCOPATED COUNTERPOINT

The rules of Counterpoint are very strict. In harmony, consecutive octaves and fifths are forbidden. In Counterpoint, it is a major offense even to approach a fifth or an octave from the same direction. Chords, too, are under all kinds of restrictions, and six-four chords, for instance, are banned altogether in strict Counterpoint. These restrictions make Counterpoint a rather exacting exercise, but for this very reason, contrapuntal practice is as good for musical self-discipline as strenuous athletics are for bodily health.

HAYDN'S CANON ON A DOG'S DEATH

∽IO∽

Themes and Voices

NOW that we are familiar with the meaning of Counterpoint, we may probe a little deeper. Our main interest lies in the Fifth Species of Counterpoint, in which individual voices move about in rhythmic freedom. A well-constructed contrapuntal composition is like a gathering of lively but well-mannered people. The conversation is maintained in groups, but when one of the guests has something important to tell, the others tone down their conversation in order to hear him. In music, when one voice has the theme, the other voices furnish polite Counterpoint.

One of the most effective contrapuntal devices is imitation. The principal speaker presents a Theme. After he has finished, someone else takes it up, repeating the Theme, note for note. In the meantime, the speaker has something new to say. The second voice picks up this new musical phrase and imitates it again, while the first speaker makes still another musical statement. The imitator picks that one up, too, and the dialogue goes on indefinitely. This is called a Canon. The word, Canon (which, of course, must be spelled with one n) means a rule, and the rule is: Follow the Leader.

Canons may be composed in words or syllables, as well as in musical notes. For the sake of variety, let us build "vowel chords," consisting of different vowels. Here is a sentence which makes a fairly good three-part word Canon, even though it makes little sense. Try it in a speaking trio, enunciating each syllable very clearly.

FIRST VOICE:	Oh!	I	know	you	are	a	fine	boy!	
	One	for	all	is	now	all	for	one,	etc.
SECOND VOICE:	Oh!	I	know	you	are	a	fine	boy,	etc.
THIRD VOICE:			Oh!	I	know	you	are,	etc.	

The combination of different vowels produces something like a musical chord. In fact, scientists have long discovered that there is music in our speech. In the Chinese language, the same word has a different meaning, depending on the tune of the syllables. For instance, Fu means husband when it is spoken on a high note; fortune, if it goes up a minor third; office, if it rises from a low note to the fifth above; or wealthy, if it falls down a fifth.

The easiest way to compose a Canon is to write a Theme around the tonic triad. When the second voice picks up that Theme, the first voice supplies a Counterpoint, rhythmically different from the theme, but based on the tonic triad to preserve harmony. Then the third voice comes in with the original Theme while the second voice has the Counterpoint, and the first voice has a new Counterpoint to that Counterpoint. All these Themes and Counterpoints must be in harmony with the Tonic triad. After the last voice has had its say, the original Theme comes back in the first voice, and the Canon starts all over again. Such Perpetual Canons are called Rounds, because the voices go round and round, and come back to the starting point after completing their musical circle. Among such Rounds is the old English song, *Summer Is Icumen In,* written seven hundred years ago. Another round, known the world over, is the French canon, *Frère Jacques.*

If you are mechanically inclined, make two concentric discs—one smaller than the other—and pin them together in the center. Draw a five-line music staff around the rim of the discs, and write out a Perpetual Canon like *Frère Jacques.* Rotate the smaller disc on the pin, and adjust it so as to get the proper entrances of the second, third, and fourth voices. This will give you a vivid representation of the musical Round.

$\mathcal{O}$II$\mathcal{O}$

Cross-note Puzzles

WRITE the word CHOICE in plain capital letters, turn it upside down and put it in front of the mirror. It will still spell CHOICE. This phenomenon is due to the fact that the letters in the word CHOICE are invertible. Other invertible words are BEE, OX, and BED. In fact, any word spelled with the letters B, C, D, E, I, K, O, and X will be invertible in the mirror. Try to make up words with these letters, and they will read the same in the mirror when turned upside down.

In music, too, there are chords and melodies, and even complete musical pieces that are invertible. Take the G major triad in the treble clef, G, B, D. Turn it upside down, and it will still be a G major chord. The G major six-four chord in open harmony, D (below the first line), B (on the middle line), and G (above the top line) is also upside-downable. Add another G two lines below, and a D two lines above the music staff, and you will have a still bigger G major chord which will also be invertible!

There is a violin piece in G major, ascribed to Mozart, which is invertible in a marvelous sort of way. It can be played by two violinists across the table, one reading the right side up, and the other upside down. The extraordinary thing is that the piece comes off in perfect harmony. Just imagine the difficulties of composing such a piece! The first bar must agree with the last bar turned upside down; the second bar should similarly harmonize with the one before last in mirror reflection; the middle bar should be the accompaniment to itself upside down, and the two players, meeting in the middle of the page, should continue to play in opposite directions until the end without disrupting the harmony.

Take the following sentence: Fantastic Light Danced on Moving Soldiers. Now read it backwards. The result has a quite different meaning: Soldiers, Moving On, Danced Light Fantastic. But there

THIS PIECE CAN BE PLAYED UPSIDE DOWN AND RIGHT SIDE UP AT THE
SAME TIME, RESULTING IN PERFECT MOZARTEAN HARMONY

are also sentences that come out the same when read backwards, as for instance, All For One And One For All. Read it backwards: no change.

In music, such reading in reverse is known as a Crab Walk. Here I should like to tell a story. A dictionary editor asked the famous French naturalist, Cuvier, to pass on a description of a crab as "a red fish that walks backwards." Cuvier replied that the definition was perfect except that a crab is not red, unless treated in boiling water; it is not a fish, but a crustacean, and it walks sideways, not backwards. But despite Cuvier's authority, the crab is still popularly supposed to be walking backwards, at least among musicians. Great composers

PLAY THIS PIECE UPSIDE DOWN. IT WILL COME OUT THE SAME
AS RIGHT SIDE UP.

have amused themselves by writing crab compositions in which the melody is read backwards. There are also Canons in crab movement. In such crab Canons, voices imitate the principal theme backwards. Sometimes the composer makes it a little harder by giving such baffling instructions as, "The crab goes forth whole, and comes back in halves." This means that the theme is to be played backwards in its entirety, and then repeated twice as fast, halving the note values.

One modern composer wrote an orchestral suite describing a Frankenstein monster. In this suite the last movement is a crab imitation of the first movement. The first movement portrays the creation of the monster, and the last movement pictures its destruction. Then there is an opera named *To and Fro*. The action in this opera goes on normally until the middle, and then is put in reverse, like a moving picture film run backwards. In the first part of the opera a lady receives a letter, and is subsequently murdered by her husband. The body is carried off the stage, and the opera ends, or rather arrives at the point when the crab movement begins. Then the body of the wife is brought in backwards through the door, and comes back to life. She seals the open letter and returns it to the servant who had originally handed it to her. This is the end, or rather the beginning, or both end and beginning.

One might ask: Why indulge in such strange practices? After all, music is supposed to contribute something to the appreciation of beauty. Well, great poets have amused themselves by writing poems with tricky rhymes, and this has never interfered with their true inspiration. So why should musicians deprive themselves of a little relaxation by way of composing invertible and mirrorable melodies?

✥12✥

What Is a Fugue?

A GIRL student who was told by her teacher to buy Bach's Fugues, could not read the name correctly, and asked a clerk in the music shop for Batch's Fudge. It took him some time to figure out what she meant, but she got her Fugues in the end.

> There was a young woman named Hatch
> Who was fond of the music of *Batch*.
>   It isn't so fussy
>   As that of De*bus*sy.
> Sit down, I'll play you a snatch.

Most music students know how to pronounce Fugue correctly, but how many know what a Fugue is made of? The word Fugue comes from the same root as fugitive, for a Fugue is literally a flight of themes. First, there is an opening statement, without accompaniment, in a single musical line, in a single musical voice. This statement, the Subject, or in Latin, *Dux,* is then picked up in another voice in the Dominant, a fifth higher, or a fourth lower. This restatement is the Answer, or in Latin, *Comes,* a companion. While the Answer is played, the Subject supplies an accompanying figure, the Countersubject. Then another voice enters, in which the Subject is repeated an octave lower, or an octave higher, depending on the order of entrances of voices. These entrances and re-entrances continue until all the voices have had their say, either as Subjects or as Answers. This concludes the first part of the Fugue, the Exposition.

Then comes the Development, with the voices playing the theme in various keys, in free imitation. The tension grows. New entries do not wait for the theme to finish, but intrude ahead of time. This telescoping of voices is called the Stretto, which means narrowed, squeezed. After the Stretto, the Subject is sounded once more in the Tonic, and the Fugue comes to an end on a full Tonic chord.

Among special tricks one has to learn in a Fugue, is the so-called Tonal Answer. According to tradition, the Tonic must be answered by the Dominant, and the Dominant by the Tonic. But there are five notes from the Tonic to the Dominant, and only four notes from the Dominant to the Tonic, so that the first five notes of the scale must be answered by the four upper notes, with the Tonic answering both the Subdominant and the Dominant. According to the rules of the Tonal Answer, a theme based on a major triad, C, E, G, is answered not by G, B, D, but by G, B, and C.

Here is a simple rule for making up a Tonal Answer: Transpose the Subject a fifth higher, or a fourth lower. This is a Real Answer. If there is a Supertonic in that Real Answer, replace it by the Tonic, without changing any other note in the Answer. The result will be a Tonal Answer.

Let us illustrate the Tonal Answer by a verbal analogy. Suppose you play a game in which your partner must repeat a short sentence replacing the word Me by You. Me, being a rather important personal pronoun, is the Tonic. You, being second in importance to Me (for people are selfish) is the Supertonic. When Me occurs as a syllable in another word, it is also replaced by You. Now let us make up a sentence with Me in it: "A Fugue is merely a special form of Canon." The Tonal Answer to this is: "A Fugue is *yourely* a special form of Canon." Here is another sentence: "A Fugue has the same meaning in music as a perfectly designed Gothic arch has in architecture." The Tonal Answer to this is: "A Fugue has the same *youning* in music as a perfectly designed Gothic arch in architecture."

Let us find a Tonal Answer to the following Subject in G major: D, G, B, F sharp, G, B. You can figure it out even without actually playing the theme, by transposing the letter-notes a fifth up in the musical alphabet, and then replacing the Supertonic, which is A in G major, by the Tonic, G. The Real Answer is A, D, F sharp, C sharp, D, F sharp. The Tonal Answer will be G, D, F sharp, C sharp, D, F sharp, with only one note changed.

A Fugue may contain two or three subjects, each having its own Exposition and its own Development. Such Fugues are known as Double or Triple Fugues. Bach's G major Fugue from the first book of the *Well-Tempered Clavichord,* is a Double Fugue of a very interesting structure. In it, the Second Subject is the melodic inversion of the first. It is a mirrorable inversion. Turn the music upside down and put it in front of a mirror. The first Subject will then come out as the Second, and the Second as the First. It is no accident that this mirrorable Double Fugue should be in G major, for as we know, the G major triad is an invertible mirrorable chord in the treble clef. Compose your own Fugue in a looking glass!

BACH'S MIRRORABLE FUGUE

It is interesting to point out that the Bach Fugues in the *Well-Tempered Clavichord* are alternately major and minor. The first, the third, and all odd-numbered Fugues are in major, and the even numbered Fugues are in minor. The first Fugue is in C major, the second in C minor, the third in C sharp major, the fourth in C sharp minor, and so on. This arrangement makes it possible to name the number of a Fugue if you know the key, and vice versa. If the Fugue number is divisible by 2, it is in minor; if not, then in major. Let us find the key of Fugue No. 15. Being an odd number, it must be in major. To find the key, we must divide the number by 2, ignore the remainder, and count up the number in the quotient, which is 7, in semitones from C. Seven semitones up from C is G, so the Fugue No. 15 must be in G major. For minor keys, we must divide the number by 2, subtract 1 from the quotient, and count the resulting number in semitones from C. For instance, Fugue No. 10 will be in a minor key, 5 minus 1 semitones up from C, which makes it in E minor.

To find the number from the key, reverse the process. Count up the semitones from C to the keynote of the Fugue, multiply the number of semitones by 2, and add 1 if the Fugue is major; or add 2 if it is minor. For instance, the Fugue in E flat major is No. 7, because there are three semitones from C to E flat, and 3 multiplied by 2 plus 1 equals 7. If you are interested in numbers, this calculating exercise will stimulate your imagination.

Although Bach's Fugues look forbidding and ultrascientific, their Subjects and Countersubjects are very lively. Ebenezer Prout, who was a great Bach scholar, wrote some amusing lines to go with the Bach Fugues from the second book of *The Well-Tempered Clavichord*. The Subject of the Fugue No. 10 was set to these words: "As I rode in a penny bus going to the Mansion House, off came a wheel, down went the bus, and all the passengers fell in a heap on the floor of the rickety thing." The Fugue No. 12 inspired Ebenezer Prout to write the following (and the words fit the subject of this minor-key Fugue very well indeed): "I told you you'd have a stomach-ache if you put such a lot of pepper in your tea." The twenty-second Fugue drove him to despair, to judge by the words he wrote for the Subject: "Oh, dear! What shall I do? It's utterly impossible for me to play this horrid Fugue! I give it up." And the chromatic Countersubject of the same Fugue is even more expressive: "It ain't no use! It ain't a bit of good! Not a bit, no, not a bit!"

ᏽ13ᏽ

Shapes of Musical Pieces

WE HAVE learned a good deal about the tools of music, scales, intervals, chords. Now let us consider the shape of a musical composition as a whole. The shortest musical piece consists of two musical phrases, a musical question, and a musical answer. In classical music, the question corresponds to the Dominant, the answer to the Tonic. Suppose our musical question is C, E, G. The musical answer to this is G, E, C. These musical sentences are like the question: "Is it so?", answered in the affirmative: "It is so!"

We may enlarge this two-phrase form to a three-phrase composition, by making the affirmative statement first: "It is so!" Then comes a doubt: "Is it so?", followed by a resounding reaffirmation: "It IS so!"

Simple as these musical phrases are, they are the seed of all great music, sonatas, symphonies, concertos. The first part of a musical piece progresses from the Tonic to the Dominant, with all kinds of detours on the way. The second part returns from the Dominant to the Tonic, also after numerous episodes and incidents. If a composition is in three sections, it may begin on the Dominant and proceed to the Tonic. Many well-known melodies start on the Dominant—*The Star-Spangled Banner, The Marseillaise,* and *Dixie.*

Listening to simple classical music, we can learn to anticipate endings of a musical phrase, and to tell in advance whether the music would go in the direction of the Dominant or the Tonic. This will give us true appreciation of musical form. We will begin to feel musical sentences, and musical paragraphs, and we will know that the perfection of musical form depends on the correct proportion of these musical paragraphs. If a musical sentence is too long, we cannot grasp its meaning. If it is too brief and abrupt, then the music leaves no impression.

The best illustrations of simple musical forms are presented by classical dances, such as the Minuet, the Gavotte, and the Gigue. Let us examine their structure. The Minuet is in 3/4 time, and contains three sections, of which the first and the third are identical. The Gavotte is in 4/4 time, and it is also in three sections. The middle section of the Gavotte is often called the Musette, which is the French word for Bagpipe, and indeed the Musette has a drone sound characteristic of the Scotch bagpipes.

The Gigue is in 6/8 time, and is played very fast. There are only two sections in a Gigue, the first going towards the Dominant, and the second towards the Tonic. The word Gigue comes from the English Jig, a fast sailor's dance. Closely related to the Gigue in its rhythm is the Tarantella, a quick Italian dance in 6/8 time. There is a story that the name Tarantella comes from tarantula, a poisonous spider. The playing of the Tarantella was supposed to cure those bitten by the tarantula. However, nobody ever tried to play the Tarantella in a hospital when a tarantula victim was brought in.

National dances are different in rhythm and melody, and yet they all possess a symmetric form that breaks up naturally into two or three parts. Take for instance, the Waltz and the Polka. The Waltz is in 3/4 time, and it is usually formed in a chain of little waltzes, each one in three musical phrases. The Polka is in 2/4 time, and is built of two-phrase themes. In both dance forms, the Waltz and the Polka, the Tonic and the Dominant alternate fairly rigorously, and it is rare that the melody should go into unrelated keys.

Though the Polka is derived from a Polish word meaning a Polish girl, the dance itself is of Bohemian origin. And no one knows the reason why the spotted design on materials used for women's clothes is called Polka Dot. Among genuine Polish dances, the Mazurka is the most characteristic in its rhythm, which has an accent on the second beat in 3/4 time. The word Mazurka comes from the Mazur Lakes in Poland. Then there is the Polonaise, which in its concert form was glorified by Chopin. The word Polonaise is the adjective of *La Danse Polonaise,* a Polish dance.

In Spanish dances, two rhythms combine, 3/4 time and 6/8 time. 3/4 time has three beats, and 6/8 time has two beats in a measure. When the melody is in 6/8 time and the accompaniment in 3/4 time, as happens in Spanish dance music, there is a cross accent in the middle of the bar which lends the music its peculiar charm.

Latin American music is greatly influenced by the Spanish rhythms. Furthermore, such popular dances as the Rumba and the Samba keep something of the jungle in their dash and color. Here we cannot talk about formal symmetry and progressions from the Tonic to the Dominant and back. The rhythm reigns supreme in Latin American dances, and the form remains only as a container to be filled with fluid musical gold.

Closely related to dance forms is the classical Rondo. It may be in any rhythm at all, 2/4, or 6/8 or 3/4 or 4/4, but it is usually played in a rapid tempo. In a Rondo, musical phrases overlap and the principal theme returns time and again with slight variations. In between, there are new themes and melodies. Perhaps the best idea of the Rondo can be given by interlocking your fingers. The fingers of your left hand will represent the melodic forms of the principal theme, and the fingers of the right hand will be the different new themes. A Rondo may be very long because you can always introduce new themes or new variations of the principal theme.

When a musical seed grows, each cell divides into several cells, forming new musical organisms. A good composer manages to maintain unity among all these microscopic—or shall we say musicoscopic—particles, so that when we listen to the complete composition, we imagine something round, with the musical center at an equal distance from all the various episodes and passing melodies.

ᏭᎦ14ᏭᎦ

The Ways of a Sonata

OF ALL musical forms, the Sonata is the most respectable, and has the best pedigree. Yet, in its essence, the story of a Sonata is simple. It can be told in two lines:

On to the Dominant
Back to the Tonic.

The word Sonata means something sounded or played. It may be played by a solo instrument, as a Piano Sonata, or by two instruments, as a Sonata for Violin and Piano. But for some reason, when a composition in Sonata form is played by three instruments, it is no longer called a Sonata. It is a Trio. Such are the strange ways of musical terminology.

Another paradox is that a Sonata usually has four movements, of which only the first is in Sonata form. In that first movement, there are two themes, the first one lively, and the second, slow and songful. The first theme is in the Tonic, the second in the Dominant. This concludes a section called the Exposition, in which the two principal themes are exposed or exhibited. In classical Sonatas, the Exposition is repeated. The repeat is indicated by a double bar with dots, the repeat sign. It occurs about one-third of the way of the first movement, and the very presence of the double bar at this point is in itself a hint that the composition is a Sonata.

After the Exposition, comes the Development. In it, the themes appear in various keys, related and unrelated. Then the Dominant is sounded powerfully in the bass, and remains there for quite a while. This bass note is the Pedal Point. This name comes from the church organ, which has a set of foot keys arranged in a regular scale, with sharps and flats. Feet are *pedes* in Latin, and foot keys are therefore called pedals. The organ pedals are huge in comparison with the piano, and look like the keyboard of a giant.

To return to our Sonata, the Pedal Point marks the transition to the final section, the Recapitulation. It contains the same two themes as the Exposition, only the second theme is played in the Tonic, instead of the Dominant. The first theme is as a rule in the Tonic, too. Sometimes (as for instance in Mozart's famous Sonata in C major), the first theme is given in the Recapitulation in the Subdominant key, and the second in the Tonic.

After the Recapitulation, there is a musical epilogue, the Coda. The word Coda means a tail, and the Coda forms the tail-end of a Sonata. There are flourishes and brilliant arpeggios played freely, and written without bar lines. These ornaments are called Cadenzas. In classical Sonatas, the Coda ends with a number of repeated Tonic chords. It often happens at piano recitals that the audience begins to applaud before the final chord, and the pianist gives his public an angry look as if to say: "Can't you wait till I am through?"

The story of a Sonata may be told in the form of a world tour. Suppose we designate continents and islands as chords and keys. Let North America be the Tonic, or Home Key, and South America, a Relative Key. For instance, if the United States is in the key of C major, South America will be A minor. Let us call Europe the Dominant, for indeed Europe is the dominant factor in world politics. Africa is situated right underneath Europe, and ought to be named the Subdominant. Asia is in the middle of the globe, and should be named the Mediant. Australia is the Submediant because it is under Asia. On the world map in Mercator's projection, Greenland looms large above the North American continent, and may therefore be called the Supertonic, seeing that America itself is the Tonic. The islands of the Arctic Ocean are marked as Remote Keys. For instance, in C major, a remote island like Spitzbergen may be in E flat major or in F sharp minor. Modulation from continent to continent and island to island is effected by sea, and the Atlantic, the Pacific, and the Indian Oceans will therefore be christened Modulation Oceans.

In our Sonata tour, we shall start off with a survey of the United States, the Home Key. This domestic tour will be the first theme of the Exposition. Then we will cross the Modulation Ocean to Europe, where we will sound off the second theme, in the Dominant. The European trip will conclude the Exposition. The next part of our tour will be taken up by the Development. We will take side trips to Asia, Australia, or board a plane for the Remote Keys to watch the midnight sun in F sharp minor. Or else we may take a sight-seeing tour of South America, in the Relative Keys.

THE MAP OF A SONATA

Having covered the surface of the globe, we naturally begin to feel homesick. At the last port of call, the steamship gives out a long whistle, on the Dominant. This is the Pedal Point. All aboard! We cross the Modulation Ocean and land on the hospitable shores of the Home Key. This is the Recapitulation. The first theme is played in the Tonic, and the second theme, also in the Tonic. Then there is a festive gathering. Stories of adventure are told and retold in a Coda. There are after-dinner speeches, and unscheduled appearances, the Cadenzas. Our Sonata tour is concluded on a series of Tonic triads.

Let us not forget that a single movement of a Sonata—usually, the first movement—covers all this territory. But a classical Sonata contains four movements. The second movement is a songful air, which forms an excellent contrast to the excitement of the first movement. Then follows a stately Minuet, or a light Scherzo. The word Scherzo literally means a joke. In actual composition, a Scherzo is a lively movement in 3/4 time, with a distinct middle part, which is often called a Trio. Why a Trio? Because in old music, the main part of light dance forms was played by two instruments, one for the melody, and one for the bass. The middle part added one more instrument, making it a Trio.

The last movement of a Sonata is a Rondo, with the principal theme alternating with new musical material. Often, this Rondo assumes some aspects of a Sonata form, in which case it is called a Rondo-Sonata. In this hyphenated form, there are two distinct sections, one in the Tonic, and one in the Dominant, as in a Sonata, but they are embedded in fresh musical material, as in a Rondo.

In animal life, there are creatures like the Australian anteater that are mammals, and yet lay eggs. In music, too, there are intermediate forms that are neither Sonatas nor Rondos. After all, music is a living art. Why should composers be less versatile in their creative output than anteaters?

Musical Arithmetic

MUSIC has its history and its geography, and also its arithmetic. A simple theme of a few notes may be developed by means of musical arithmetic into a full-fledged concert piece.

Let us learn Musical Addition. Suppose you wrote a melody like this (the semicolon after G stands for a rest):

```
―――――――――――――――――――――――――――――――――――――
          A
―――――――――――――――――――――――――――――――――――――
               G;
―――――――――――――――――――――――――――――――――――――
                              E
―――――――――――――――――――――――――――――――――――――
                                  D
―――――――――――――――――――――――――――――――――――――
C                                              C
```

Using Musical Addition, we can prettify this melody so that it will look like this:

```
―――――――――――――――――――――――――――――――――――――
            b
―――――――――――――――――――――――――――――――――――――
          A
―――――――――――――――――――――――――――――――――――――
               G;
―――――――――――――――――――――――――――――――――――――
                                    f
―――――――――――――――――――――――――――――――――――――
    e                         E          e
―――――――――――――――――――――――――――――――――――――
                                  D
―――――――――――――――――――――――――――――――――――――
C                                              C
```

The small letter-notes are the ones that have been added. In this Musical Sum we can still recognize the original melody. Such musical sums are called Variations, because they introduce variety into a musical theme. In old Spanish music, Variations were called Differences, a very fine and poetic name which is worth reviving. How nice it would be to compose a Theme with Differences!

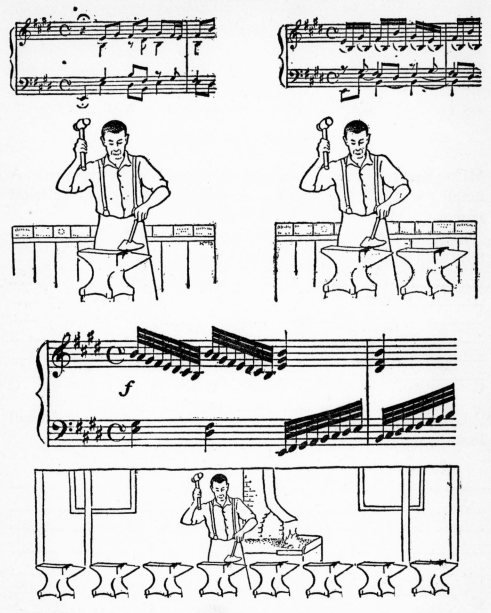

THE HARMONIOUS BLACKSMITH MULTIPLYING HIS ANVILS

Readers of Dickens will recall Pip in *Great Expectations*. He served as a blacksmith's apprentice, and was nicknamed Handel by his friend, Mr. Pocket, whom he met in Chapter XXII. "We are so harmonious," said Pocket, "and you have been a blacksmith . . . Would you mind Handel for a familiar name? There's a charming piece of music by

Handel, called *The Harmonious Blacksmith.*" Pip heartily agreed, and went by the name of Handel for the rest of the novel.

The Harmonious Blacksmith is a set of variations. The harmonious effect is attained by the blacksmith through a very simple system of Musical Multiplication. In the theme there are two strikes on the anvil for every quarter-note. In the Variations, the rhythm is musically multiplied so that there are four notes, six notes, or eight notes to a beat.

A melody can be multiplied by playing it in thirds, in sixths, or in octaves. Beethoven, in his C major Sonata, multiplies the scale by both thirds and sixths, so that it comes out in six-three chords. And it is difficult to play, too! Brahms likes to multiply his melodies by sixths and octaves. And Debussy is apt to present a musical phrase encrusted in chords made up of two minor thirds topped by a perfect fourth. According to this formula, C is musically multiplied to a chord containing C, E flat, G flat, and B. Play these chords on every white key, and you will get a very different effect from a simple C major scale!

What is Musical Division? The opening movement of Beethoven's *Moonlight Sonata* provides an excellent example. The chords are split into flowing arpeggios, three notes in each group. In arithmetic we check up on division by multiplying the quotient by the divisor. In Musical Arithmetic, too, we can verify the result by putting the chord together again after it has been broken up. Play the *Moonlight Sonata* with chords made up of three notes of each group, and you will obtain full harmony.

Musical Arithmetic offers another interesting possibility of making several melodies out of one. It is Musical Permutation, or Musical Shuffling. You know that you can arrange three letters of the musical alphabet in six different orders. Four notes can be arranged in twenty-four different ways. Take the notes G, C, D, and E. You can arrange these notes in six different ways beginning with G, six different ways beginning with C, six different ways beginning with D, and six different ways beginning with E. Much to your surprise, you will find that the world's most famous melodies are made up of these four notes. You will hear *The Westminster Chimes, Frère Jacques,* and *How Dry I Am.* By repeating some of the notes, you can get *The William Tell*

Overture or *Yankee Doodle*. Indeed, there is enough material in these four notes alone to keep one composing music for a hundred years.

The C sharp minor Prelude of Rachmaninoff is based on a theme of only three notes. By the process of Musical Multiplication, these three notes are magnified into one of the most effective piano pieces of modern music. Do you know how many notes there are in this Prelude?

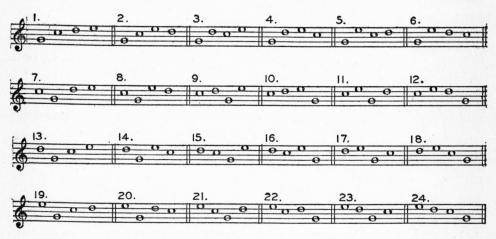

TWENTY-FOUR PATTERNS OF FOUR IMPORTANT NOTES

One thousand, seven hundred and twelve. If you can play this Prelude through without missing too many notes, ask your friends to guess the total number of notes. You will have a hearty chuckle at their expense, for they will be hundreds of notes off the mark.

The English composer Henry Purcell wrote, over two and a half centuries ago, a Fantasia with a single note as a theme. Yet, thanks to his skill in Musical Arithmetic, this Fantasia never gets monotonous, even though the word monotonous in Greek literally means "of a single tone"!

❧ 16 ❧

Telling Stories in Music

HAS music any meaning? Can one tell a story by playing a musical composition? Some musicians regard music as a telepathic language which can be understood but not explained in words. Others assert that music is akin to architecture, perfect in form, but carrying no message to the mind.

No one denies that it is possible to convey a definite mood by musical means. Mozart's music is cheerful because it is full of vivacious rhythm, and also because he wrote mostly in major keys. Tchaikovsky's music is sad and mournful, and most of his compositions are cast in minor keys. And we know that Mozart was a happy genius, even in adversity, while Tchaikovsky was a victim of constant depression, even when he enjoyed financial success and artistic recognition.

Some composers feel that emotional states correspond to definite chords and keys. Rimsky-Korsakov believed that love is in A major, and wrote love arias in his operas in that key. The Russian modern composer, Scriabin, associated each tonality with some color. C major was red, D major, yellow; A major, green; D flat major, violet; F sharp major, blue. In the score of his symphonic poem, *Prometheus,* Scriabin uses a color organ, which is supposed to project different colors on the screen, according to the changing chords in the music.

In classical music, words are illustrated by corresponding musical intervals. For instance, in Bach's cantatas, the sentence, "I shall stand firm," is expressed by the same note repeated four times. The words, "Get up, get up!", are arranged as a major arpeggio going up. In the phrase, "But it is so far," Bach uses a large interval, the minor ninth. And the words, "Lead me," are vocalized in a scale going up for three octaves.

The American composer, Roy Harris, uses the intervals from the prime to the ninth in his choral composition, *A Red Bird in a Green*

Tree, to mark the first, second, third, etc., day on which "my true love" brings gifts. On the second day she brings two silver hens, and the melody is based on the interval of a second; on the third day she presents three white crows, and the interval is a third. On the eighth day, she comes around with eight cows, for an octave, and the ninth day is the day of the nine lives of nine cats, indicated by the interval of a ninth.

BACH'S THEMES ILLUSTRATING THE WORDS

Moods are expressed in music by subtle evocation. Mendelssohn wrote a collection of piano pieces, *Songs Without Words.* The titles of these wordless songs suggest the mood of each—*Regret, Restlessness, Consolation, Hope, Agitation, Sadness, Lost Illusions.* It would be very interesting to play these pieces one after another for an audience of musical listeners, and ask them to guess which is *Consolation,* and which is *Agitation,* and which is *Lost Illusions.* Such experiments would settle the question whether music can tell a story.

Nature has been described in music by many composers. There are symphonies and symphonic poems descriptive of the oceans and the seas. Rivers, too, have not been neglected. There is the Beautiful Blue Danube in the rhythm of a waltz, and there is the Bohemian river, Moldau, in a symphonic movement by the Czech composer, Smetana.

Mountain ranges have been pictured in music, too. The most impressive piece of mountain music is the Symphony of the Alps by Richard Strauss, complete with a wind machine and a thunder machine. When the first performance of *The Alpine Symphony* was announced, a sarcastic subscriber sent in an inquiry, asking whether a rain machine was included in the score, and whether it was advisable to bring an umbrella along.

One of the most popular storms occurs in Beethoven's *Pastoral Sym-*

phony. The music itself looks stormy in the score. There are half-notes that look like rain drops, and a lot of sixteenth-notes below, resembling dark pools of rainfall.

Wars and battles are the subjects of several musical works. There is the *1812 Overture* of Tchaikovsky, which describes Napoleon's retreat from Moscow, with a real cannon included in the score. And there is a battlepiece by Beethoven, *Wellington's Victory*.

Animal sounds, the rooster's crowing, the warbling of birds, the humming of insects, have inspired many a great composer. In *The Carnival of Animals,* the French composer, Saint-Saëns, introduces elephants, turtles, kangaroos, and a swan. By courtesy, pianists, too, are included in this musical zoo. They play scales up and down!

Bird calls often figure in musical compositions. In Beethoven's *Pastoral Symphony,* there is a nightingale, singing its trills in counterpoint with a quail and a cuckoo. And the cuckoo appears solo in a piano piece by the French composer Daquin. But the most realistic bird appears in the symphonic poem, *Pines of Rome,* by the modern Italian composer, Respighi. Instead of imitating a nightingale, Respighi uses a phonograph record of a live nightingale, which is put on at the proper moment and sings its captive song to the accompaniment of muted violins.

Cats are not melodious animals, but they have provided inspiration to musicians. The Italian composer, Scarlatti, wrote a *Cat Fugue,* so named because he took the theme from his pet cat, which walked on the keys, stepping on G, B flat, E flat, and F sharp. In an ultra-modern piece called *The Anatomy of Melancholy,* the composer, whose name had better remain unmentioned, includes a special part for a cat's meow, to be produced by a live cat pulled by the tail! In order to avoid being scratched, the player is instructed to pass the cat's tail through a hole in a wooden partition. The piece was never performed for fear that the Society for the Prevention of Cruelty to Animals might have something to say about such unmusical treatment of cats.

Insects, too, have been flying in musical compositions for quite some time. There is a graceful piece by Grieg, *The Butterfly,* and there are butterflies in Schumann's music, under the French name, *Les Papillons.* The Hungarian composer, Béla Bartók, wrote a piano piece entitled *The Diary of a Fly,* which is a masterpiece of insect music. Then

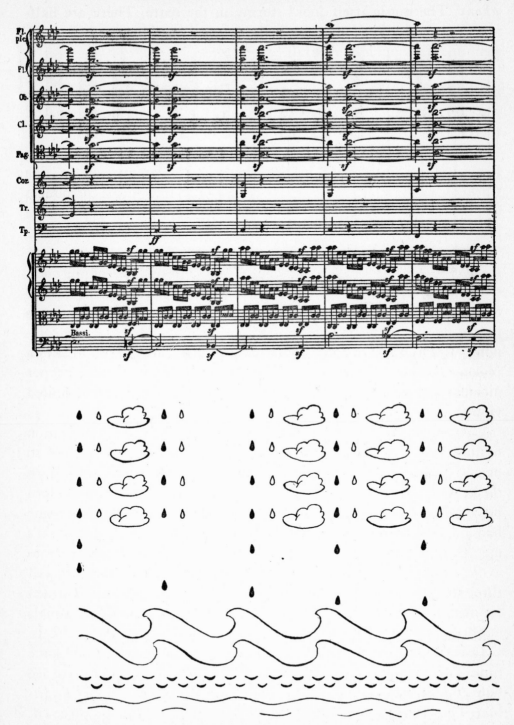

BEETHOVEN'S STORM MUSIC ACTUALLY LOOKS STORMY

(*Picture by Carl Saxild*)

THE CAT'S FUGUE

there is *The Flight of the Bumblebee,* by Rimsky-Korsakov. Do you know where this bumblebee flies, and for what purpose? The answer is: he flies home to bite his aunts. Yes, for Rimsky-Korsakov's bumblebee is no ordinary bug. He is a royal prince who was sent sailing the ocean in a barrel by his perfidious aunts. But he was a precocious child, and navigated the barrel successfully to a fairy island. There he learned magic, turned into a bumblebee, and flew back to get even with his aunts. The bites are realistically indicated by accents in Rimsky-Korsakov's music. Some scientists maintain that Rimsky-Korsakov got too many accents in, for a bumblebee can bite only once. This particular bumblebee must be an exception.

Musical inspiration may come from unexpected sources. Did you ever listen to the dripping faucet in the kitchen or in the bathtub? The dripping of the water has a definite melodic and rhythmic pattern, and can provide an interesting theme for a modern composition. The automobile horn, the jangling of milk bottles, the chugging locomotive, and other civilized noises are a source of inspiration to a musician who has his inner ear attuned to the life around him. In fact, there are several musical scores which include noise as part of music. In his score, *The Iron Foundry,* the Russian composer, Mossolov, uses a tin

GALLOPING HORSES, A CACKLING HEN, A CUCKOO, AND A
BUMBLEBEE. WHICH IS WHICH?

Answers (spelled backwards)
1. EEBELBMUB   2. NEH   3. OOKCUC   4. SESROH

sheet shaken with loud reverberation to illustrate the sounds of factory life. Then there is *The Mechanical Ballet* by the American composer, George Antheil, which employs several player-pianos and four airplane propellers. When *The Mechanical Ballet* was first performed in New York, a music critic complained that the airplane propellers blew away the notes he made during the concert and that he forgot what he intended to say about the music. Another listener put up the collar of his overcoat to protect himself against the wind.

THE MELODY OF THE FAUCET

All this is realistic music. But music may be composed by suggesting an image rather than actually imitating nature. There are paintings which look like photographs, and there are pictures that seem to hover in a blue fog, with men and objects dimly outlined, as though seen through blurring eyeglasses. There is a great charm in such blurred images, and the painter can express his own feeling of things in a more individual way by painting in this manner. In music, too, there are composers who express themselves by half-phrases, like an unfinished dialogue: "Would you, then . . . ?" "Oh yes, of course. But how could we . . . ?" "Oh, no, I did not mean it in this way . . ." Listening to such a scene in a play, we cannot tell what the actors are talking about, and yet we receive a very strong impression of something that is happening somewhere. Musical impressions may be equally suggestive. The greatest composer of Impressionist music, that is music that suggests a scene without actually pointing its finger at it, was Debussy. In his piano piece, *Clair de Lune,* he paints moonbeams in D flat major, so delicately that we can barely guess at the meaning of the music. As in the game of charades, we can gradually surmise that the music describes a calm landscape, suffused in light, pale, even light. What light is pale, even, and very white? Why, the light of the moon, or *Clair de Lune* in French. Most of Debussy's music conveys impressions of quiet or mysteriously blurred images: *Steps in the Snow, Mist, Dead Leaves, Wind in the Valley.*

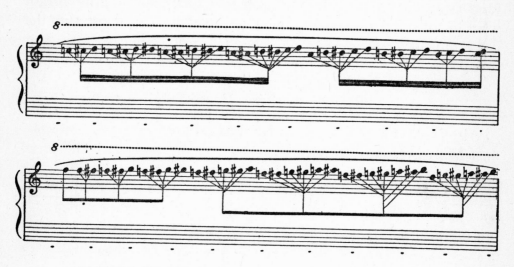

CLUSTERS OF NOTES THAT LOOK LIKE CHERRY TREES
(FROM *Night of Dreams* BY JAIME PAHISSA)

Musicians, as a rule, have a fine sense of humor, and like to play practical jokes in music. Debussy once had a bet with the pianist, Harold Bauer, who was a great admirer of Wagner, that he would make Bauer laugh at Wagner in public. Debussy was at that time writing his piano suite called *Children's Corner,* and Bauer was to give its first performance. So, very slyly, Debussy used a theme from Wagner's opera, *Tristan and Isolde,* in the last movement of his *Children's Corner, Golliwog's Cakewalk.* Immediately after the Wagner quotation, Debussy put in a laughing musical phrase, ha-ha-ha, ha-ha-ha. Bauer never realized that this was a quotation from Wagner, and he unsuspectingly performed the piece at his concert. Then Debussy told him the secret. Bauer did laugh at Wagner in public, and Debussy had won his bet.

Mozart once wrote a piece which he called *A Musical Joke,* and in it he used consecutive fifths, the whole-tone scale, and all kinds of forbidden musical progressions—forbidden in classical music, of course. Mozart's *Musical Joke* ends in five different keys simultaneously. But in modern music such an ending is no longer a musical joke. It has a long name—Polytonality.

DEBUSSY LAUGHS AT WAGNER

Also in a humorous vein are such musical pieces as *A Chess Game,* in which chess moves are imitated by melodic intervals. The pawn moves two spaces, and the melody moves two degrees of the scale. The knight jumps obliquely, as knights do in chess, and the melody moves an augmented fourth up. When the bishop dashes off on a diagonal, the music imitates the move by a rapid scale passage. Play this piece for a chess expert, and the chances are he will name the moves without a slip.

A MUSICAL CHESS GAME

Even atoms have been pictured in musical compositions. The modern composer, Edgar Varese, has written a piece called *Ionization,* scored for drums, rattles, anvils, and two fire-engine sirens. In case you are not sure what Ionization means, it is the state of electrical conductivity of the air induced by the presence of radioactive substances. Anyway, it is something about knocking off the atoms. And certainly Varese's music sounds ominous, now that we know what atoms are up to. He wrote *Ionization* fifteen years before the atomic bomb, and that is a musical prophecy!

The Brazilian composer, Villa-Lobos, invented a system of composition from charts and photographs. He transfers the outline of a picture on special squared paper, and reckons one square to a semitone of melody. When the line goes up so many squares, the melody goes up the same number of semitones; if the curve goes down, so does the melody. In this manner Villa-Lobos set to music the New York skyline, with skyscrapers playing very high notes. He has also transcribed a picture of the author of this book at the breakfast table, with wife and child. The melody is not very attractive, but Villa-Lobos could not help it. He did his best with the material at hand.

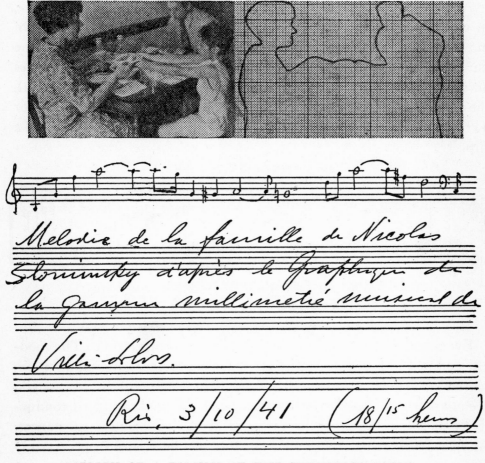

MELODY OF A FAMILY AT THE BREAKFAST TABLE

ᒛ17ᒐ

The Rainbow of Overtones

HAVE you ever wondered why a note played on the piano sounds differently from the same note on the violin or some other instrument? The difference lies in the tone color, a musical rainbow formed around each sound, like a halo over a street lamp on a foggy night. These overtones cannot be readily heard, but they can be brought out into daylight by means of resonance, a musical echo.

You are familiar with the workings of the loud and soft pedals of the piano. But do you know what the middle pedal is for? When you play a note and step on the middle pedal, it holds up a little damper over the string, leaving it free to vibrate.

Make this experiment. Press down the following notes in the middle of the keyboard, C, G, C, E, and G. Then step on the middle pedal. Now strike a low C in the bass, rather vigorously, several times over. You will perceive an ethereal harmony, a chord of overtones. These overtones come from the strings liberated by the middle pedal. They were present in that low C all the time but they were too weak to be heard. When we release the dampers of the strings corresponding to the overtones, C, G, C, E, and G, these notes vibrate by resonance. It is the same resonance that makes the china rattle when you sing a note to which it happens to be attuned.

There is a story about an opera singer whose voice was so powerful that he broke the bathroom mirror by singing while shaving. So if you have a voice rich in overtones, better forbear from singing in the bathroom!

To prove that all these overtones are really present in the low C, let us repeat the experiment in reverse. Press down the low C without striking the key, and step on the middle pedal. That will keep the C string free to vibrate. Now strike the Overtone Chord, C, G, C, E, and G, and let go at once. The Overtone Chord will continue to sound, not on its own strings, but in the low C string.

Try similar experiments with other notes. In every case, the Overtone Chord will form a major triad, with the Tonic and Dominant doubled. Indeed, the major triad is the only natural chord in music.

The Aeolian Harp hung on a tree will produce the overtones of a major chord when the wind sets the string in vibration. A real aerial

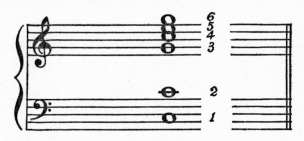

THE OVERTONE CHORD

harmony can be produced by sending up a paper kite with a string stretched across the frame. And this harmony will be an arpeggio in a major key.

With a little patience, you can learn to hear overtones even without bringing them out by resonance. Play a note in the middle register of the piano, and release it instantly. You will hear the octave sound lingering for a brief moment. Attune your ear to a high G while striking C, and pretty soon you will be able to hear it without much trouble. Listening to overtones is a fascinating experience which will give you a new appreciation of music.

You can play overtones even on a single string. Open the lid of the piano, and let the index finger of your left hand glide from the middle of the string towards the dampers, while playing the corresponding note on the keyboard. You will hear a bugle call. By adjusting the rhythm, you will soon learn to play the army calls—a reveille, a retreat, a mess call, or a sick call—all on a single string.

The shorter the string is, the faster it vibrates. You can actually see these vibrations when you snap an elastic band between your fingers. You can feel the loudness of vibrations by pressing your hand against the radio loud-speaker. The musical waves from your favorite radio program will caress, tickle, or blow.

The highest note on the piano has the shortest string. The lowest note has the longest string. The latter is also the thickest string. Every time you go down an octave, the string is doubled in length. However, about five octaves down, the strings are made thicker, for if you kept doubling the strings all the way down, the piano would be too long for the living room. But thickness compensates for length, and so the lowest notes can be made of convenient length.

We know now that a string twice as short as another produces the sound an octave higher than it does. But what about the fifth, the fourth, and other intervals? How much shorter or longer should the string be to produce a sound a fifth higher, or a fourth lower? We can learn these numbers from the Overtone Chord, because it so happens that this chord corresponds to the natural division of a string into two, three, four, five, or six sections, all vibrating at the same time.

Let us play the Overtone Chord with the low C, which we will call the Principal Tone, because it generates the rest of the overtones as a beam of white light generates a rainbow when it breaks up into colors. Let us put a number on each of these overtones, from the bottom up. The bass will be No. 1; the next C will be No. 2; G will be No. 3; C, No. 4; E, No. 5, and G, No. 6. Let us tabulate the ratios of vibrations for each interval in the Overtone Chord.

Octave	2/1
Fifth	3/2
Fourth	4/3
Major Third	5/4
Minor Third	6/5

By inverting the major third, we can obtain the ratio for a minor sixth, which will be 8/5 (we have to multiply the denominator 4 in the ratio for a major third by 2 in order to bring it up an octave for the inversion). We can get the ratio for a major sixth by inverting the minor third. The result will be 10/6, or 5/3. Indeed, we find this major sixth between No. 3 and No. 5 in our Overtone Chord.

It is not necessary to memorize these ratios, which are the magic numbers in the science of music. All you have to do is to play the Overtone Chord, and call out the numbers for each interval. It is no more difficult than counting sheep on your fingers. But if you feel that you are confused, take this drastic measure: stick gummed labels on your fingers, No. 1 on the little finger of your left hand; No. 2 on the thumb of your left hand; No. 3 on the thumb of your right hand, No. 4 on the index finger of your right hand; No. 5 on the fourth finger, and No. 6 on the little finger of your right hand. Then play the Overtone Chord using these labeled fingers. To find the magic numbers, all you need to do is to read the labels for whatever interval you select. This method is absolutely foolproof.

The knowledge of magic numbers will enable you to name the number of vibrations for any note on the piano. Musicians tune their instruments by middle A, which has 440 vibrations per second. The A an octave above has twice as many vibrations, that is 880 vibrations. The A above has twice 880 vibrations, that is 1760 vibrations, and the A an octave above that A has 3520 vibrations.

The A below the middle A will have one-half as many vibrations as the middle A, that is 440/2 or 220 vibrations. The next A below will have 110 vibrations; the A an octave below that, 55 vibrations, and the lowest A on the piano, 27½ vibrations.

Using our magic numbers, let us figure out the number of vibrations for C sharp, a major third above A. The magic number for a major third is 5/4. The number of vibrations for A is 440. In order to find out the number for C sharp, we must multiply 440 by 5/4, which results in 550. So C sharp has 550 vibrations per second.

Let us find the number of vibrations for E above A. The magic number for a fifth is 3/2. Multiplying 440 by 3/2, we get 660. So the E above the middle A has 660 vibrations per second. From E we can find the number of vibrations for G by multiplying 660 by the magic number for a minor third. Combining these ratios, we can find numbers of vibrations for all notes of the scale. There may be a slight difference in those numbers, depending on whether we go by thirds or by fifths, and from where. To tell the truth, our fifths and thirds on the piano are not quite pure, and their magic numbers are slightly off.

This is a matter that concerns piano tuners. Play a fifth, A to E, in the middle of the keyboard, and listen carefully. You will hear a strange whooshing sound wave going up and down, louder and softer, like this, oooooOOOoooooo. These pulsations or beats show that fifths on the piano are not pure fifths. Only the octave is a pure interval on the piano, and when you play the octave, there are no beats. But on the violin, fifths are tuned exactly according to their magic number, and so are the fifths on other string instruments. The reason for the whooshing fifths on the piano lies in the tempered pitch, in which the octave is divided into twelve equal semitones. In doing so, we have to chip off a vibration or two from our fifths, and add some vibrations to other intervals.

Have you a violinist among your friends? If so, tell him to play an octave above his G string, and ask whether he places his finger nearer to one or the other end of the string. Whatever answer he gives, he will be wrong. His finger has to be exactly in the middle of the string in order to produce an octave sound, and few violinists realize that. Your knowledge of the magic numbers will enable you to perform a magic trick, namely, to tell the violinist the exact distance, to a fraction of an inch, from his finger to either end of the string. All you need to know is the length of a violin string, which is thirteen and a half inches. In order to play an octave, the violinist has to place his finger at 6¾ inches from either end.

If you possess the precious gift known as absolute pitch, you will be able to name the distances in inches for whatever note your violinist friend chooses to play. Remember only that the higher the sound, the shorter the string, and it is shorter by as much for each interval as the magic number. You must understand it very thoroughly before attempting the trick. For instance, if the violinist plays a note a major third above the open string, G sharp on the E string, or C sharp on the A string, he has to make the string 5/4 times shorter, which means that his finger will be placed on the point four-fifths of the length of the string. For C on the G string, the magic number is 4/3, and so the playing portion of the string will be three-quarters of its entire length.

Imagine the amazement of your violinist friend when you name distances for all these notes with 100% accuracy, as he can easily find out by measuring them with a ruler.

You can perform the same feat on the viola or the cello as well. All you need to do is to measure the length of the strings on these instruments. The rest is accomplished with a little headwork on figuring out your fractions.

∞18∞

Music Pleasant and Unpleasant

SOME intervals and chords have a satisfying finality, like a full stop in punctuation. Then there are chords that sound like a question mark, or a dash, and demand a continuation. The pleasing and satisfying intervals and chords are called Consonances, the displeasing ones, Dissonances. Consonances are made up of intervals in the Overtone Chord —the octave, the fifth, the fourth, the major third, the minor third, the minor sixth, and the major sixth. Seconds and sevenths, and all augmented and diminished intervals are Dissonances.

If a chord has even one dissonant interval, it becomes a Dissonance. This does not seem to be a reasonable arrangement, but such is the stern musical law. Like a fly in the ointment, one second or a seventh spoils an otherwise perfect Consonance.

But the interesting thing about Consonances and Dissonances is that the sound alone does not decide the matter. The same chord, spelled differently, may be either a Dissonance or a Consonance. The word Soul sounds the same as Sole, but Soul is our noblest self, while the sole of our foot is the lowest.

Even a C major chord may under certain conditions become a Dissonance. Play the following notes in rapid arpeggios, E flat, B flat, D flat, G, B flat, D flat, and F flat, with the pedal on. Then play a C major chord in the middle register of the piano. It will actually sound like a Dissonance, a chord that has to be resolved, just as a question mark has to be followed by an affirmative sentence. C will want to come down to B flat in order to satisfy our inner ear. To tell the truth, this is not a C major chord at all. It should be spelled with an F flat to conform with the rest of the notes.

Play the E major scale in the right hand, and the C major scale in the left. All the intervals will be major thirds, and yet the double scale will sound extremely strange to our ears. So here is an example of

87

C MAJOR CHORD THAT SOUNDS DISSONANT

Consonances that sound like Dissonances. Some Dissonances may be made to sound like Consonances if they are arranged in a special order. Play a chain of seventh-chords and their inversions on the white keys, beginning with the Dominant Seventh chord, and going through the Tonic Seventh, the Subdominant Seventh, the Leading-Tone Seventh, the Mediant Seventh, and so on, finally ending on the Tonic. Of these chords, only the very last is a Consonance, the rest being Dissonances. Yet the impression is rather pleasing to the ear. Why? Because all these chords belong to the familiar key of C major, and we anticipate a satisfying conclusion on the Tonic triad. So here are Dissonances that behave like Consonances. No wonder George Gershwin, the American composer who made popular music into a distinctive art, said: "Discords make the sweetest airs."

DISSONANCES THAT SOUND PLEASING TO THE EAR

Dissonant intervals normally resolve into Consonances. Let us see how to resolve a seventh. Play middle G on the piano with the index finger of your left hand, and play F above this G with the index finger of your right hand. Move the index finger of your right hand from F down to E. This will be the resolution of a seventh into a sixth. Now cross your hands, placing the index finger of your right hand on F below G, and holding G with the left hand. It will be an inversion of the seventh, which is a second. F will still move down to E, so that the resolution of a second is a third. The reason for using your index fingers and crossing the hands is that such a method will show you clearly how the inversion of a dissonant interval resolves into the inversion of the resolution.

A seventh resolves into a sixth by moving the upper note down. Therefore, the inversion of a seventh, which is a second, resolves into the inversion of a sixth, which is a third, by moving the lower note down. A good way to remember the resolution of a second is to play Chopsticks, in which F goes down to E.

Let us resolve an augmented fourth, which is a Dissonance. It will go to a sixth, by moving the upper note up and the lower note down. For instance, F to B is an augmented fourth, and it will resolve to a sixth, by moving F to E, and B to C. Perform this resolution with the index fingers of both hands, and then cross hands and invert the interval, by playing B below F with your right hand. The resulting interval will be a diminished fifth, which will resolve into a third. F will still go to E, and B will still go to C. In the first movement of Beethoven's *Pathétique* Sonata there is a whole row of augmented fourths and diminished fifths resolving into sixths and thirds, in C minor.

Now let us consider the case of an augmented sixth. It sounds the same as a minor seventh, but we know that the spelling changes the meaning of intervals and chords. A minor seventh from C is B flat, while an augmented sixth from C is A sharp. The augmented sixth resolves into an octave. The upper voice moves a semitone up, and the lower voice a semitone down.

A Dominant Seventh chord which contains a minor seventh may be respelled with an augmented sixth. Such a respelling is called an enharmonic change. The poet, Robert Browning, described the resolution of a chord with an augmented sixth in verse:

And music: what? That burst of pillared cloud by day
And pillared fire by night, was product, must we say
Of modulating just, by enharmonic change,—
The augmented sixth resolved,—from out the straighter range

Of D sharp minor,—leap of disimprisoned thrall
Into thy life and light, D major natural?

There are several augmented and diminished intervals that resolve
in this very forceful way, by moving inward or outward, and always
in semitones. These are one-way Dissonances, and they give us this
anticipation that Browning suggests in his verse. The augmented sixth
resolves outward by semitones into the octave. So the inversion of the
augmented sixth resolves inward by semitones, and into a unison. A
doubly augmented fourth, as for instance C flat and F sharp, resolves
outward into a major sixth, C flat going to B flat, and F sharp going
to G. Its inversion, a doubly diminished fifth, resolves inward, into a
minor third. You can easily verify this by playing inversions and resolutions with crossed hands.

*The augmented sixth resolved—from out the straighter range
Of D sharp minor—leap of disimprisoned thrall
Into thy life and light, D major natural*

(*Robert Browning*)

But what was a Dissonance yesterday may be a Consonance today.
In modern music and jazz, a piece often ends on a dissonant chord,
such as the Tonic seventh chord, C, E, G, B. The Russian composer,
Scriabin, constructed a chord of six notes, C, F sharp, B flat, E, A,
and D, which he declared to be a higher Consonance. This chord is
known as the Prometheus Chord because Scriabin used it in his symphonic poem, *Prometheus,* which portrays the legendary hero who
stole fire from heaven and was punished by the gods by being chained
to a rock.

In our democratic age, the restrictions against free use of Dissonance
are gradually dropped. Dissonances are used without resolutions, and
chords are built that look like skyscrapers. In classical music we stop

at the ninth-chord, G, B, D, F, and A. By adding another third on top of the ninth-chord we obtain an eleventh-chord. Still another third will form a thirteenth-chord. This is as far as we can go, for the fifteenth-chord will duplicate the bass note, like this: G, B, D, F, A, C, E, G. But if we use all the twelve notes of the chromatic scale, then we can reach a chord of the twenty-third. This is how to arrange it in a chain of thirds: G, B, D, F, A, C, E flat, G flat, B flat, D flat, F flat, A flat. This is a remarkable chord, for it contains four different triads, two major and two minor ones, which use up all the twelve chromatic tones.

There are chords even more complicated than the chord of the twenty-third, for instance, a chord with all twelve different notes and eleven different intervals, from a minor second to a major seventh.

Amusingly enough, you can solve the problem of building such a chord by experimenting with a clock. Suppose you have to do eleven errands on condition that each errand should take a different number of even hours, from one hour to eleven hours, and that you should finish each errand on different hours of the clock. You start at 12:00 noon, and complete your first errand in one hour, at one o'clock. Then you do the next errand which will take you two hours, and which you will complete at three o'clock. The third errand taking three hours will be finished at six o'clock, and the fourth at ten o'clock. But you cannot do your fifth errand in five hours, because you will then finish it at three o'clock, and you had already covered three o'clock at the completion of your second hour. Of course, all this does not take into consideration that you are a human being and cannot run errands one after another for hours on end. In this clock game you are a robot who never tires.

Believe it or not, there are hundreds of ways of arranging these errands without duplication of the hour or the length of each errand. The musical point of the clock game is that you can regard the twelve hours of the clock as twelve notes of the chromatic scale, and the length of each errand as a musical interval. Here is one solution: Run your errands in the following order of hours: 11, 2, 9, 4, 7, 6, 5, 8, 3, 10, 1. Try it over on your clock. Then try it on the piano, counting semitones instead of hours. You will get the following chord: C, B, D flat, B flat, D, A, E flat, A flat, E, G, F, and F sharp.

This has been christened The Grandmother Chord, for its progeny includes every member of the chromatic scale and every distance of musical kinship. You cannot play The Grandmother Chord on the piano unless you have six fingers on each hand, and hexadactylism (here is a big word to look up in a big dictionary) is extremely rare among musicians.

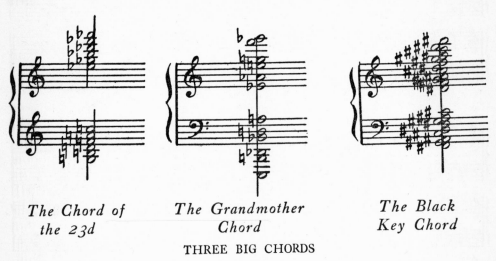

The Chord of   The Grandmother   The Black
  the 23d   Chord   Key Chord

THREE BIG CHORDS

When we do gymnastics, we often contort our bodies in a way that hardly seems normal. But by so twisting our limbs we acquire a great liberty of body control. In music, too, we often learn how to do tricks in order to obtain perfect control of the technique of composition. There is a very important school of composition in twelve tones estab lished by Arnold Schoenberg. According to his system, you build your themes out of twelve different notes. Naturally, there is no definite key, no definite tonality, and all the twelve chromatic tones are democrati cally equal. For that reason, this type of music is sometimes called Atonal Music. It is very easy to learn to compose Atonally. Write the names of the twelve chromatic notes on twelve cards and shuffle the cards. Then copy the notes as they come out, using different octaves and wide intervals. The result will be an Atonal melody.

Another device much used in modern music is Polytonality, mean ing many tonalities, just as polysyllables mean words of many syllables. Play a tune in C major with an accompaniment in F sharp major. The result will be a Polytonal harmonization.

Ach, Du Lieber Augustin

IN ATONAL, POLYTONAL, AND PANDIATONIC SETTINGS

To round off our vocabulary, let us mention the Pandiatonic system of composition. Diatonic music is our familiar music, based on major and minor scales, and the word Diatonic means going through tones, just as the word Diameter means running through or across the circle. Pandiatonic is all-diatonic, just as Pan-American is All-American. Pandiatonic harmony is a free harmony on white keys, which makes use of dissonant and consonant intervals at will. Children banging on the white keys of the piano often produce interesting Pandiatonic effects. In modern music, Pandiatonic harmony is used to add spice to the common C major tonality, and the result is not at all unpleasant.

❧19❧

Fiddles, Horns, and Drums

MUSICAL sounds are produced by all manner of means, by blowing a horn, bowing the violin, or striking the keys of the piano. But each instrument has its own tone color, as easily recognized as the familiar voice of a friend.

Every nation in the world has its own popular instruments, the Spanish guitar, the Russian balalaika, the Scotch bagpipe, the American banjo. And there are other strange instruments—the voodoo drums of Haiti, and the nasal flutes of Paraguay, actually played through the nose, and the giant mouth harmonicas of Bolivia, reaching ten feet in length.

But we are not concerned here with these unusual and exotic instruments. Let us account for those used in symphony orchestras and bands. There are string instruments, which include violins, violas, violoncellos, and double-basses. There are wind instruments—flutes, oboes, clarinets, bassoons, horns, trumpets, trombones, tubas, and saxophones. And there are percussion instruments, including drums, bells, and gongs. There are also plucked instruments like the harp, and keyboard instruments like the piano or the xylophone.

A French poet duplicated the sound of the violin in a wonderful line, *"Les sons longs de violons."* This is the romantic violin that plays a luscious melody in the stillness of an evening. But the violin can also play very fast, at the rate of a thousand notes a minute. A violin has four strings, all of the same length, but of different thickness. These strings are tuned in fifths, G, D, A, and E. By pressing a little harder on the strings with the violin bow, the player can perform double notes on two neighboring strings. And he can dispense with the bow entirely, and pluck the strings with the tips of his fingers. This guitar-like playing on the violin is called pizzicato, the Italian word for plucked.

George Gershwin once wrote a humorous song in which he described how four famous Russian violinists, named Jascha, Toscha, Mischa, and Sascha, began to fiddle when they were three years old, but their "tone was sour, until a man, Professor Auer, came right along, and taught us all how to pack 'em in Carnegie Hall." Professor Auer was also the man who used to say: "Break the fiddle over your pupil's head, tear up his music, but send him home with a hope in his heart." Incidentally, the Russian word for the violin is *Skripka,* which means a screecher!

The lowest sound that the violin can produce is G below middle C. When lower notes are needed, they are given to the viola, which is also tuned in fifths five notes lower, C, G, D, and A. Both the violin and the viola are "chin instruments," for they are held under the chin, with the left hand, while the right hand manages the bow. String instrument players use only four fingers of the left hand for all their scales and melodies, but these four fingers have to be acrobatically agile to perform all the difficult violin music that is written for the instrument.

The viola parts are written in the alto clef, which has middle C on the third line. The senior colleague of the viola in the family of string instruments is the violoncello, or cello for short. Its parts are written in the bass clef, or in the tenor clef. The four strings of the violoncello are an octave lower than those of the viola, C, G, D, and A. It is easy to remember that the lowest cello string is C because the word cello begins with the letter C. Just say C for Cello, and you will never forget it.

The violoncello is a leg instrument, and is placed between the knees. Its sound is sonorous and powerful in the low register, songful and lyrical in its melody range, on the A string. Like the violin and the viola, the cello can play double notes and produce pizzicato effects by plucking the strings.

The lowest of the string instruments is the double-bass, disrespectfully nicknamed the bull-fiddle or the dog-house, because of its bulky size. The player has to sit on a high stool, or stand beside the double-bass, in order to operate it. The strings of the double-bass are tuned in fourths, E, A, D, and G. The lowest string E is a sixth below the C of the cello. It is easy to remember the order of the double-bass strings, because it is the reverse of the violin, E, A, D, and G, instead of the violin strings G, D, A, E. The double-bass is the least glamorous among string instruments. In most cases, it merely supports the cello by underplaying its part an octave lower. And the double-bass does not participate in the string quartet, which is made up of two violins, a viola, and a cello.

Now let us take up the blowing instruments. Flutes, oboes, clarinets, and bassoons are usually referred to as wood-wind instruments, even though modern flutes are often made of metal. The horns (or as they are more fully known, French horns), the trumpets, the trombones, and the tubas belong to the brass section, even though they may be made of some other metal alloy. A further complication is that jazz players call the trumpet a horn, and there is even a book, *A Young Man with a Horn,* which is about a trumpet player in a jazz band. And nobody knows why French horns are called French.

The gentlest wind instrument is the flute. It simply cannot play too loudly. In fact, the flute player does not blow into the instrument, but across it, like blowing over the top of an open bottle. And some inexperienced flute players do sound as though they were blowing over an empty bottle, rather than across the flute.

The lowest note of the flute is middle C, and the flute can produce about three octaves, or a little over. It is important to remember that all musical instruments have a fixed lower limit, but their upward range may be extended by a few notes by skillful playing. In the wind instruments, the range of three octaves is the average, but the oboe and the trumpet cannot get beyond two and a half octaves.

The flute family has a junior member, the piccolo. The word piccolo means the little one, and indeed the piccolo is the tiniest thing. The player can carry it in his vest pocket. The piccolo can play a whole octave above the flute, and it is as shrill in the upper reaches as a crying baby. In fact, the piccolo can go as high as the highest C on the piano, while a crying baby seldom reaches F sharp below high C, even during the worst tantrums.

The oboe is the very opposite to the flute in its character. Its voice is deep and penetrating. The player has to squeeze the airwaves through a double reed, which forms the mouthpiece of the oboe, and the result is a fluttering sound, as though emerging from a narrow opening of a subterranean cave. Someone has called the oboe a philosopher among

musical instruments. Philosophers think deeply and speak in measured phrases. So does the oboe playing a solo. But at other moments,
the oboe may be simple, poetic, and lyrical in its musical speech.

The lowest note of the oboe is B flat below middle C. To remember
this, notice that the first musical letter-note in the word oboe is B, and
B in the German musical alphabet is our B flat. Incidentally, in German the oboe is called hobo, but of course this word does not carry the
American meaning. The oboe is anything but a hobo.

The range of the oboe does not extend over two and a half octaves,
and its high register should be used sparingly. The flute can go on
playing for a long time without taking a rest, but the oboe must take
a few bars' vacation every once in a while, or else it will choke on its
own notes. The oboe can produce fast repeated notes and scales, but
it cannot compare with the flute in agility. A professor of philosophy
can hardly hope to outrun a shepherd boy.

The oboe has a senior relative, the English horn. As with the French
horn, no one knows why the English horn is so named. It is possible
that the original name for it was angled horn, from a French word
meaning bent, because the mouthpiece of the English horn is bent in
a curve. As to its musical characteristics, it sounds deeper than the
oboe, and it is best suited for pastoral music, depicting the sunrise
over the pastures and similar landscapes.

Now let us consider the clarinet, which is the most popular among
wood-wind instruments. The very word clarinet suggests clarity. Its
sound is carried on the airwaves with ease and smoothness. The clarinet can play as fast as the flute, and it can even slide up the chromatic
scale, as it does in the opening solo of Gershwin's *Rhapsody in Blue.*

If you look in the clarinet part and in the flute part of the same
piece, you will discover, to your surprise, that the key signatures are
different. If the flute plays in C major, the clarinet will have two sharps
in the key signature. But if the flute part has two sharps, the clarinet
will have one flat. Is there some hugger-mugger like Polytonality
afoot? Nothing of the sort. These different key signatures are required because the clarinet is a transposing instrument. It plays one
note, and out comes another. If its C sounds like B flat, it is a clarinet
in B flat. If, when it plays C, the actual sound is A, it is a clarinet
in A.

Suppose you happen to come across one of those old pianos abandoned in a barn for fifty years. Piano strings slacken with time, and the pitch drops. You play C major, but it sounds like B flat major. You play B flat major, but it sounds like A flat major. Everything sounds a whole tone lower. Such a piano is a piano in B flat. There is one convenience in using a B flat piano. If you happen to accompany a piece in B flat major by ear, and if you are not very expert in playing music with black keys, then a piano in B flat is your meat, if one may say so. The American composer of popular music, Irving Berlin, has had a special piano constructed for him which transposes into any key at will. But Irving Berlin prefers black keys to white keys, so he composes his melodies on black keys, switches the modulation crank to a desired key, and gets results without laborious trying.

When a piece is in flat keys, the B flat clarinet is used, and it saves two flats for the player. If a piece is in sharp keys, then the A clarinet is used. The key of A has three sharps, which are economized for the player in case there are more sharps. But if there are only two sharps, then the clarinet player has to have the key signature of one flat to step down from his three sharps that are provided in the A clarinet.

We have used the clock for modulation, and for other purposes, so that a clock has become to us a musical instrument, too. Let us use the clock to understand transposing instruments. The clarinet in B flat is a clock set at ten o'clock, because B flat major is two hours before zero hour. The clarinet in A is a clock set at three o' clock, because A major has three sharps. Now suppose that the time of day is two o'clock. The A clock is nearer to two o'clock than the B flat clock, so we take the A clock, and turn it back one hour to set it at two o'clock, the time of the day. In musical terms, it means that if the composition is in two sharps, we take the clarinet in A, and put a key signature of one flat. Setting the clock back one hour is putting one flat in the key signature.

The lowest note in the clarinet as it is written is E below middle C, but it sounds a tone lower on the B flat clarinet, and a minor third lower on A clarinet. The range of the clarinet is about three octaves, but jazz clarinet players can blow much higher.

The clarinet family includes a number of senior and junior members. There is a bass clarinet, tuned an octave lower, and even a double-bass clarinet, which goes two octaves lower. Then there are small clarinets, transposing upwards from C. Of these small clarinets, the best known is the clarinet in E flat, which sounds a minor third higher than the written notes.

The bassoon is the bass of the wood-wind instrument group. It has a rattling sound in quick notes, but in melodic passages it is extremely mellow. The lowest note of the bassoon is B flat below the staff of the bass clef. To remember it, say, "B flat for Bassoon," or relate the first letter of the word bassoon to the German B, which, as you know, is our B flat. The lowest note of the bassoon is two octaves below the lowest note for the oboe.

The range of the bassoon is three octaves, and it sounds well all along its course. The senior member of the bassoon family, the double-bassoon, plays an octave lower than the bassoon, and serves as a support for the bassoon, just as the double-bass supports the cello. Double-bassoon solos are rare, and not always complimentary to the nature of the instrument. For instance, in Ravel's musical fairy tale from Mother Goose, *The Beauty and the Beast,* the double-bassoon is the beast.

The flute, the oboe, the clarinet, and the bassoon, are the principal members of the wood-wind quartet. Compared to the string quartet, the flute is the first violin, the oboe a second violin, the clarinet is the viola, and the bassoon a cello.

In the brass family of instruments, it is impossible to form a quartet. The instruments will not blend. They are too aggressive for harmonious coöperation. Four French horns would make a beautiful quartet among themselves, and three trombones with a tuba will provide a majestic four-part harmony, but the trumpets will have to remain independent. The good range of the trumpet is only two octaves, from middle C to high C two octaves above. Trumpets in bands are mostly B flat trumpets, so their C actually sounds B flat. But C trumpets, which sound the same as written are commonly used in symphony orchestras. On these trumpets, the high C is entirely practicable.

The world record of high C's was set by Louis Armstrong, the famous jazz trumpeter, who hit high C 280 times in succession.

A trumpet is a powerful instrument, and on the weighing scales of musical loudness, one trumpet equals the rest of the orchestra. You remember what happened to the walls of Jericho when the trumpets blew in unison. No atomic bomb could do a better or a cleaner job. True, the Jericho trumpet had a longer tube, but there is no doubt in the mind of those whose next-door neighbors are trumpet players, that the modern trumpet is an earth-shaking and eardrum-piercing instrument.

The French horn has a more poetic name in German, the Waldhorn, a forest horn. When Carl Maria von Weber, the founder of the German romantic opera, wished to convey a feeling of the mysterious German forests, he wrote for the horns. Of all the instruments, the horns can sustain a sound the longest time. In classical music, you find in the horn part notes tied over from one bar to another, and the player is expected to carry the sound without interruption. But the French horn can also play brilliant fanfares. Its high notes are bright and clear.

In classical music, the horn was always tuned in the key of the piece, or in the Dominant, because early French horns could play only the natural overtones, which are, of course, all in one major key. For every switch of key, the player had to adjust the tubes in the horn, to make it lower or higher. Nowadays, all horn parts are written in F, which means that the actual sound is a fifth lower than the written note. And the key signature is not used in the horn part at all. Accidentals, sharps and flats are marked as they come. The range of the horn is three octaves, and it can play as high as an octave above middle C.

The trombones are the only musical instruments that are made shorter or longer while playing, like Alice in Wonderland after she drank the magic potion. Of course, we know that the longer the tube, the lower the sound. So when we see the trombone player pulling out the tubes to the limit of his arm's length, we can confidently expect a very low sound. The trombone can rarely play the lowest notes with assurance, and its best field is on both sides of middle C. The trombone is not a transposing instrument, or to put it more scientifically, it is an instrument in C. When you play C, it sounds C. As to clefs, the bass clef is most often used in trombone parts, but the tenor clef, which shows the position of middle C on the fourth line of the staff, is employed for high notes.

The underpinning prop of the brass section is the tuba, which is to the rest of the brass what the bull-fiddle is to the strings. The tuba is hardly a romantic instrument, even though Ravel gives it a solo in his orchestration of Moussorgsky's *Pictures at an Exhibition*. But do you know what picture is described by the tuba solo? The rattling horse cart!

In military bands there are numerous species of brass that are not acceptable in the high society of a symphony orchestra. There is a Sousaphone, named after the American March King, John Philip Sousa, and there is the helicon, familiarly known as the rain catcher, because its big, open-mouthed bell is directed upwards and presents an inviting target for precipitation. It is an unwieldy instrument, but it looks impressive with its shiny coils. The player wears it like the Indian poncho, thrusting his head through the central opening.

> There is a big brass called the Helicon,
> It's not fit to exhibit a relic on.
> It blows hard and loud,
> It frightens the crowd,
> It's h—l to play scales on the Helicon.

We must not forget the saxophones, which are newcomers among musical instruments. The saxophone is named after its inventor, the Belgian musician, Adolphe Sax. They are close to the wood-wind in their functions, but they are made of metal. Saxophones are not found in symphonic scores, but they are heart and soul of band music.

From the lowest note of the double-bassoon to the highest note of the piccolo, the range of musical instruments covers the entire keyboard of the piano, except the low A. Beyond these limits we cannot tell the difference between the notes. Very low tones produce a sinking sensation in the pit of the stomach, like a prelude to seasickness, and very high notes hurt the eardrums by their piercing vibrations. A few notes above the highest C, we cannot hear anything. But dogs can. There are special dog whistles, inaudible to humans, which are used by dog trainers. The trainer blows the whistle, and the dog comes running and wagging his tail, while the trainer himself does not hear a sound.

Below a certain number of vibrations per second, sound disintegrates into a series of rapid knocks. You can hear these knocks when a trolley car begins to move. As it gathers up speed, the knocks become more frequent, and soon a low, rumbling tone is heard. If you have absolute pitch, you can tell by the sound how fast the street car is going, and how soon you will get home on an F sharp or a B flat.

Strings, wood-winds, and brass are melody instruments. Drums, bells, and cymbals are percussion instruments, and they take care of rhythmic punctuation. The only percussion instruments used in symphonic music are kettledrums because they can produce definite sounds. These kettledrums usually come in pairs, playing the Tonic and the Dominant. When the symphony progresses into the development section, and modulations are made into various keys, the kettledrums are compelled to silence, because they can play only in the original key. But they come into action when the recapitulation approaches, and when the Dominant is sounded in the bass, giving one of the kettledrums an opportunity to deliver a mighty roll. And in the Coda, the kettledrums have a busy time hitting the Tonic and the Dominant over and over again.

Among drums that serve the rhythm without playing definite notes are the military drum and the bass drum. The military drum is used in march-like music, and the bass drum gives a booming roll for such musical scenes as the head of Robespierre falling into the basket after his execution on the guillotine.

Then there are metal percussion instruments—the cymbals, the triangle, the gong, and the tamtam. The gong and the tamtam are used for decorative effects in romantic music. The cymbals, which are two metal plates struck together, provide a crashing sound for such episodes as the sinking of Sinbad's ship in Rimsky-Korsakov's *Scheherazade*. The triangle furnishes a pleasant little tinkle for special effects. There is a triangle solo in Liszt's *Piano Concerto in E flat,* and for that reason, the whole Concerto is sometimes nicknamed *The Triangle Concerto.*

The harp stands by itself in the society of musical instruments. It is of the noblest and most ancient ancestry, but its modern shape is quite different from the one that King David played for King Saul. It is a graceful instrument with its triangular frame, spanned with golden strings. The natural music for the harp is made of arpeggios, for the very word arpeggio comes from the Italian word for the harp, *arpa*. But it is not as easy to play as it seems while watching a harpist's hand gliding across the strings, for every harp player must also be a tuner. Each string on the harp can play a flat, a natural, or a sharp, and the tuning is changed by means of special pedals. To play a diminished-seventh chord in arpeggios, the harpist has to tune his strings like this: B, C flat, D, E sharp, F, G sharp, and A flat. B and C flat sound the same, of course, as do E sharp and F, and also G sharp and A flat. Listening to a harp playing an arpeggio, we actually hear some notes twice, but we do not notice it because of the speed. This duplication cannot be avoided, because the harpist has to use all seven letter-notes, with sharps or flats, in order to be able to glide through his arpeggio passages. And the result looks strange in the harp part, with a confusing mixture of sharps and flats.

To complete our panorama of musical instruments, we must mention the glockenspiel, the xylophone, and the celesta. The xylophone means in Greek a wood sounder, and its keys are actually made of hard wood. They are arranged like the piano keyboard, except that only a few octaves are used. The glockenspiel is the German name for a set of metal plates giving a complete diatonic scale, exactly like the toy tinpans of the nursery. Then there is the celesta, a name suggesting heavenly music. But in point of fact, there is little celestial harmony in the tinkling sound of a celesta. And this brings up a sad story of a musician who chose the celesta as his favorite instrument.

THE MAD CELESTA PLAYER

Would you care to play the flute?
  He replied in French: *Ah Zût!*

How about the clarinet?
  He shot back in Russian: *Nyet!*

Would you then take up the cello?
  But he mumbled: *Non è bello.*

Why not try the double bass?
  He said, "No," and twitched his face.

Then he spotted the celesta,
And exclaimed in Spanish: *¡Esta!*

In this tale the saddest fact is
That in spite of daily practice,
He could not play the celesta
In fortissimo or presto.

He swore loudly in Rumanian,
Dutch, Arabian, and Iranian.
Why, he cried, did I say *Nyet*
When I heard the clarinet?
And the wonderful old cello
Is so exquisitely mellow.

In the end, the mental fester
So perturbed his soul's siesta,
That like some demented jester
He demolished the celesta.

Years have passed; his face was wrinkled.
There was silence. Nothing tinkled.
But at night, hallucinating,
He heard something fascinating,
Like a heavenly celesta
At a fabulous fiesta,
Playing forte, molto presto,
Presto,
         P r e s t o ,
                P R E S T O ,
                        P R E S T O . . . .

❧ 20 ❧

Playing Music Together

WE HAVE now acquainted ourselves with the nature of musical instruments. We know what notes they can play and what their capacities are. But how can different instruments be blended together into a harmonious ensemble? It is hard enough to march in step when the only rhythm is one-two, one-two. But in a musical composition for several instruments, each player has his own individual part which must somehow be integrated into a complete musical picture. Yet experienced musicians can perform a trio or a quartet without a rehearsal. This requires a musical instinct, a sort of a sixth sense that is a mystery to a non-musician.

True, there are general indications for the tempo and the expression in the musical score. These indications are given in Italian because Italy was the first to establish a system of musical terms. Let us review some of these terms. The word tempo itself means time in Italian, and it indicates the speed of the music. From the slowest to the fastest tempo, the Italian terms are these:

> Adagio
> Lento
> Andante
> Allegro
> Presto
> Prestissimo.

When the music is to be played faster, it is marked Accelerando; when slower, Ritardando, or Ritenuto.

For expression marks, from the softest to the loudest, the words are these:

> Pianissimo
> Piano
> Mezzo forte
> Forte
> Fortissimo

LENTO   ANDANTE   ALLEGRO   PRESTO

When the music is to be played louder, the word is Crescendo, or growing; when softer, Diminuendo, diminishing.

Tempo marks give a rather vague idea of the actual speed of playing. But there is a way to fix the tempo with precision, by a musical time machine called the metronome, which word literally means the measure law. The metronome clicks off beats with an upward pendulum which swings from 40 to 208 beats a minute. The metronome speed can be adjusted by shifting a movable weight on the pendulum. Suppose the composer wants to mark the speed at one second for every quarter-note. He writes: a quarter-note equals M. 60, the letter M. being of course the abbreviation for metronome. For the tempo twice as fast, the metronome mark is 120, which means 120 beats to a minute, or two beats to a second. For intermediate speeds, numbers between 60 and 120 are used. And of course, the composer may give the metronome mark for an eighth-note, or for a half-note, or for a dotted quarter-note at any tempo between 40 and 208 beats a minute.

Your heart is a pretty good metronome. The tempo of your heart solo is Allegro Moderato, and the metronome mark of your heart-beats, unless you get excited, is seventy-two.

But even the metronome will not help a musician who is in the habit of slowing up after a few minutes. The metronome is all right for practicing, and it is helpful to start a piece at the right speed, but one cannot play music with the metronome beating time throughout the performance.

There was a young lady from Rio
Who wanted to play Handel's Trio.
Her skill was so scanty,
She played it Andante,
Instead of Allegro con brio.

In playing music together, it is very important to play strictly in time with the rest of the group. There is a story about a member of a string quartet who asked a famous musician how he liked the tempo. "Fine," he replied, "particularly your tempo." It took the poor fellow some little time to appreciate the biting point of this remark.

One may be very good in mathematics and still be poor in rhythm. Einstein, the genius of modern science, is also an amateur violin player. One evening he played Mozart's sonatas with the pianist, Schnabel, who was annoyed at Einstein's poor sense of rhythm. "Can't you count?" he exclaimed impatiently. "It is so simple—one, two, three, four—one, two, three, four!"

The social sense in music is sufficient for duets, trios, quartets, quintets, and sextets. But when the number of players is large, someone must take the lead, and indicate time with a nod of his head, or with a swing of the violin bow. In olden days, one of the players assumed this role of a leader, but with the appearance of symphonic ensembles, musical conducting became a separate profession. Musical ensembles without a conductor are called chamber music, that is, music to be played in a chamber, in a room. Music played with a conductor is orchestral music, and when an orchestral group is represented by all kinds of instruments, it becomes a symphony orchestra.

The conductor stands in front of the orchestra and indicates with the motion of his hands the tempo, the degree of loudness or softness, and the shape of the musical phrase. Each conductor has his own way of telling the orchestra in gestures what he wants the players to do with the music, but there are certain definite rules about beating time. The first beat of the measure is always conducted downwards, and the last beat upwards. In 2/4 time, there is only one downbeat, and one upbeat. In 3/4 time, the beats are down, right, and up. In 4/4 time, the conductor beats down, left, right, and up. In 6/8 time, the conductor beats two to a bar, if the tempo is fast, and all six beats in a slow tempo, always remembering that the last beat should be an upbeat.

In modern music, there are time signatures with five, seven, or eleven beats to a bar. And how would you like to beat 2/8 time with the left hand, and 5/8 with the right hand? This is what the conductor has to do in one modern composition, in which half of the instruments are written in 2/8, and the rest in 5/8. In this double time, the right hand has an upbeat at the end of the 5/8 bar while the left hand beats down. It is as tough as patting your head and rubbing your stomach in different directions at the same time.

Piano music is written on two staffs, but an orchestral score has to have as many lines as there are different instruments in the orchestra. The wood-wind instruments are on top, the brass in the middle, and the strings on the bottom of the page. The violins are split into two sections, first and second violins. The expression, "to play second fiddle," comes from playing in the orchestra, or in a string quartet. And there is a story about a Russian grand duke who came to a rehearsal of the czar's orchestra, and asked why the violins were seated in two groups. The conductor explained to him that they were first and second violins. "What?" exclaimed the grand duke. "Second violins in the Imperial orchestra? All must be first!"

The conductor's business is to keep his eye on all these musical lines in the score and his ear on the orchestra. He is the switchboard operator who keeps the musical trains running on time. He must give signals to musicians when their turns come, and he must bring out the important themes. Some conductors use the baton, others direct the music with bare hands. The left hand is the expression hand, with which the conductor shows changes in loudness and softness. The *Pathétique Symphony* of Tchaikovsky ends on a gradual diminuendo which reaches such a point of pianissimo that the sign for it has four P's, PPPP, and the conductor must somehow make PPPP different from either PPP or PPPPP.

The great Italian conductor, Toscanini, has a way of showing crescendo and diminuendo by spreading out the index and the middle fingers of his hands, touching them by the fingertips to imitate the actual signs for crescendo and diminuendo as they are written in the score.

Conductors have been called autocrats of the baton, for indeed, some of them, and not the best ones, come to think that they make all the music with their hands, while the players produce none. An attempt was made in Russia to dispense with conductors altogether, for why should there be bosses in a musical democracy? A conductorless orchestra was accordingly established in Moscow, and carried on successfully for several seasons. But then it was found that too much time was wasted on decisions in matters of tempo and expression. So a conductor was elected by the players, to lead the orchestra on the basis of mutual respect and coöperation.

Associated Music Publishers

AN ORCHESTRAL PIECE BY ANTON VON WEBERN THAT TAKES
ONLY NINETEEN SECONDS TO PLAY

❦ 21 ❧

Symphonies, Rhapsodies, and Concertos

THE word Symphony means sounding together. It has the same first syllable as the word sympathy, which means feeling together, and the same ending as the word telephone which means distant sounding. The word phonograph means sound writing, and gramophone means writing sound. So we see that Symphony is related to a number of words having to do with sound. But in music, Symphony means something more than mere sounding together. It has to sound harmoniously, with orchestral instruments all blending together in a perfect ensemble.

In classical music, Symphony is a Sonata for orchestra. Like a piano or a violin Sonata, a Symphony is cast in four movements, of which only the first is in Sonata form. The second movement, in piano sonatas, as well as in symphonies, is a slow air with variations. Then comes a lively Scherzo. And for the conclusion, a symphony has a brilliant Finale, which may be in the form of a Rondo, with the main theme popping up here and there, while between times there are attractive instrumental episodes.

Although a symphony orchestra includes the word Symphony in its official title, it does not limit itself to performances of symphonies. There are other orchestral compositions, Overtures, Symphonic Suites, Symphonic Poems, Rhapsodies, and Concertos. The word Overture means an opening, and indeed symphonic programs often open with the performance of an Overture. A Symphonic Suite is, like a suite of rooms in a swanky hotel, a row of musical apartments, each fully equipped with melody, harmony, and rhythm. Just as in a luxurious hotel suite there is a drawing room, a bedroom, and a vestibule, so in a symphonic suite its separate numbers have different functions—to amuse, to entertain, or to lull to musical sleep. In a classical suite, the movements are composed of a succession of old-fashioned dances, a stately Minuet, a lively Gavotte, a sparkling Gigue. In modern music, each number of a *Symphonic Suite* may bear a picturesque title. Tchaikovsky's *Nutcracker Suite* consists of fairy-tale dances, *Waltz of Flowers, Tea Dance, Coffee Dance,* and *Dance of Candies.*

A Symphonic Poem in music is the same as a romantic ballad in literature. In a ballad there is romance, drama, and often tragedy. In a Symphonic Poem all these elements are present in music. There is a foreboding introduction, which suggests danger and apprehension, with the strings playing a tense tremolo, and the French horn, muted (the player actually puts his fist into the bell of the horn for a mute, and this for some mysterious reason not only mutes the horn, but lowers the sound by a semitone) intones a sinister call. The drums perform a spine-chilling roll. Then a clarinet or a flute plays a romantic solo, representing the feminine character in the poem. The male counterpart comes in the trumpets, or even the trombones. And so the listener is told a musical story, with all the suspense of a thrilling narrative, and yet without a single clue as to what actually goes on. Of course, the composer may name his Symphonic Poem after some well-known work of literature, and so give away the secret. Tchaikovsky wrote a symphonic poem, *Romeo and Juliet,* after Shakespeare, which tells the moving story of the unhappy lovers. Richard Strauss put philosophy into the form of a Symphonic Poem in his orchestral work, *Thus Spoke Zarathustra,* the name of the title being that of a legendary Persian philosopher. Rimsky-Korsakov's orchestral work *Scheherazade,* has elements of a Symphonic Suite and a Symphonic Poem. There are four movements which describe tales of the *Arabian Nights,* but these movements are symphonically connected by the main theme, which characterizes Scheherazade, the clever wife of a cruel Sultan who was in the habit of putting his wives to death. Scheherazade told the Sultan 1001 tales of romance and suspense, and he became so intrigued with this serial that he could not possibly behead her when she said, "continued on page so-and-so" for 1001 consecutive Arabian nights.

The Rhapsody is the latest newcomer to the symphonic field. It was made famous by Liszt in his *Hungarian Rhapsodies.* In a Rhapsody, the only rule is the rule of contrasts. Themes and rhythms follow one another in rapid succession. There are prolonged cadenzas, that is, passages in arpeggios and scales played in the manner of improvisation, with rhythmical adlibbing (adlibbing is a colloquial phrase from the dignified Latin expression *Ad libitum,* which means "as you like").

The most remarkable modern Rhapsody is Gershwin's *Rhapsody in Blue.* The Blue in the title refers to the rhythm of the southern Blues, and the "blue note" is a lowered seventh of the major scale, like B flat played in C major. In this Rhapsody, Gershwin introduced American rhythms for the first time in a "highbrow" composition. That, of course, was embarrassing to the critics, who thought that the vernacular idiom in a symphonic composition was in bad taste, something like saying "ain't" or using a double negative. But in the course of time, and a very short time, too, symphonically speaking, *The Rhapsody in Blue* became a classical American work, and is now popular not only in America, but in Europe as well.

What about a Concerto? Surprisingly enough, the word Concerto originally meant a contest. When Brahms wrote his Concerto for violin and orchestra, a critic sarcastically remarked that it should be called a Concerto for the violin *against* the orchestra, because the orchestral accompaniment was too heavy for the poor four-stringed violin to contend with. In the literal sense of the word, this is what a Concerto is supposed to be, with the soloist struggling for survival, coming to the surface, and then going under. A Double Concerto is a twin contest, soloists struggling with each other, and in addition holding their own against the orchestra. And there are Triple Concertos and Quadruple Concertos. As a matter of fact, there is nothing shocking about the idea of this musical struggle, for, as we know, all good counterpoint consists of musical ups and downs, and classical Concertos use a lot of fighting counterpoint.

In modern Concertos, manners are more polite, and there is less counterpoint, and more harmony. The orchestra keeps down when the soloist plays the theme, and comes into its own when the solo instrument displays pyrotechnics loudly enough to be heard.

The piano, the violin, and the violoncello are the principal soloists in classical and modern Concertos. But there are also Concertos for the clarinet, and the flute, and even the double-bass. And there are freak Concertos, like the Concerto for a marimba and orchestra. A marimba is a Latin-American xylophone, with dried tropical fruits suspended under each key for resonance.

A talented American composer, Norman Dello Joio, has written a unique Concerto for a mouth harmonica with a symphony orchestra. And another young American has composed a Concerto for a whistling soloist and orchestra.

Although the soloist is always the winner in the contest of a Concerto, the orchestra has the privilege of opening the hostilities. The orchestral introduction may be only a few bars in length, or it may last fully five minutes. There is a story about a Russian violinist who had a very busy season playing different Concertos with different symphony orchestras. At one of his appearances, when he was scheduled to play Beethoven's Violin Concerto (or so he thought) he held his violin leisurely in his left hand, waiting for the orchestra to begin, for there is a long introduction in Beethoven's Concerto. Imagine his surprise when the orchestra struck the first chord of the Violin Concert by Mendelssohn, which gives the violinist barely a few seconds to begin his solo. He was as quick-witted as an experienced automobile driver who suddenly notices a cat or a dog darting right across the road. He instantly threw his violin into position, and played his opening measures as if nothing had happened. But afterwards he made it a rule to inquire what particular Concerto he was to play at each of his numerous appearances!

᭒22᭒

Grand Opera, Operetta, and Ballet

WHEN instruments play together, they form a trio, a quartet, or a symphony. When voices sing in an ensemble, they make up a chorus. When singers combine with an orchestra, in a stage spectacle, with scenery, costumes, and action, the result is grand opera.

The opera as a distinctive art was born in Italy three hundred and fifty years ago, when a group of noblemen and artists gathered in Florence and decided to try a revival of ancient Greek drama, with music. The early operas were nothing more than suites of arias, alternating with spoken dialogue. The subjects were taken from classical mythology, or from the Bible. Religious operas, performed without costumes and without scenery, developed into a special form of vocal composition called Oratorio, from the Italian word meaning a place of prayer. Another form of a choral composition is a cantata, which means a piece to be sung. Cantatas may be religious, historical, or dramatic. There are cantatas on the subject of Abraham Lincoln, and cantatas about World War II, about airplane pilots, and about factories and industries.

Italy gave birth to the opera, and Italy still holds the lead in operatic production. Out of ten operas produced in the leading opera houses of the world, nine are by Italian composers, and out of ten famous opera singers, nine are of Italian origin. Italian is the most convenient of all languages for singing, because all Italian words end on a vowel that can be sung with the mouth open, and not with a consonant, as in German or English, which makes it difficult to sustain the sound. Also, all words connected with the opera are Italian, beginning with the word opera itself, which means work. These opera words are used in all languages without a translation, Solo, Aria, Libretto (which means a little book), Impresario (manager), Maestro (which means teacher), and the names of voices, Soprano, Mezzo-Soprano, Alto,

Contralto, Tenor, and Bass. The double Italian word Prima Donna, which means a leading lady, is often used ironically about people with an exaggerated sense of self-importance.

Italian opera achieved its greatest triumph in the nineteenth century with the appearance of such operatic geniuses as Verdi, Rossini, and Puccini. So effective and melodious are Italian operas, that we are willing to overlook their confusing and incredible plots. In one opera for instance, the commander of an invading army divulges military secrets to his sweetheart, who turns out to be the enemy king's daughter, and the king himself listens from behind a palm tree, carefully memorizing the names of the places which are to be attacked. In another opera, conspirators sing in perfect harmony with their intended victims, separated from them by a brick wall. Or, the operatic heroine, suffering from tuberculosis, is sturdy enough to sing for twenty minutes in the last act before succumbing to her malady. And in still another opera, Count Riccardo, billed as Governor of Boston (!) is stabbed to death by his secretary over the love of a lady.

Italian operas abound in murder and suicide. Heroines throw themselves into the bay of Naples, or stab themselves, or drink poison. In Puccini's opera, *Madam Butterfly,* the heroine commits suicide by hari-kari. Few operatic sopranos commit murder, which is the business of tenors and basses, but Tosca, in Puccini's opera of the same name, murders the brutal official with a kitchen knife after dinner.

Italian operas are violent and passionate; French operas are romantic and often sentimental. German operas are profound, philosophical, and very, very long. The one Teutonic exception was Mozart, whose operas are light and gay, written for entertainment and pleasure. But Mozart was an Austrian, not a German.

Richard Wagner, the towering master of German opera, was a contemporary of Verdi, but the two might as well have lived on different planets. Verdi wrote attractive melodies, and arranged his arias and choruses in convenient, perfectly shaped musical forms. Not so Wagner. His idea was to unite all arts in his operas, stage action, text, voices, and the orchestra. He did not even want to call the product opera, but preferred the name music drama. If Italian plots seldom make sense, Wagner's librettos, which he wrote himself, make so much sense, are so involved, philosophical, and profound, that it takes considerable effort to understand the developments on the stage, even when following the printed text. Wagner took his subjects from Germanic myths and legends, with gods, supernatural creatures, and amazing humans intermingled in continuous action. Wagner assigned to each character a musical theme, identifying him for future reference. These leading motives, as they were called, are further combined in a highly ingenious counterpoint. For instance, when Wotan surrounds one of the Valkyries, the flying horsewomen of the German legend, with a wall of fire, there is a slumber motive, and the motive of fire, the theme of Wotan himself, and the motive of her supplication, as well as fragments of other themes that appear like footnotes in a learned treatise.

No wonder Wagner could not be understood by his contemporaries, brought up on the easy music of the classics. In a contemporary cartoon, Wagner's music is represented by a huge orchestra which includes goats and jackasses, and seven cats marked A, B, C, D, E, F, G, while the conductor, suspended in midair, beats time with both hands and feet. On the podium lies an orchestral score with the title page marked: "Wagner, Not To Be Played Much Till 1995!" The author of the cartoon has been proved quite wrong, because much before 1995, Wagner's operas became part of the regular repertoire, and at least one of his melodies—the *Wedding March* from the opera, *Lohengrin*—is known wherever couples are married with a musical setting.

Those who did not like Wagner turned for relief to the French opera, such as *Carmen,* by Bizet, telling the exciting story of a Spanish working girl who made the soldier, Don José, desert the army, and then left him for the Toreador, the bull-fighter. Incidentally, there is no such word in Spanish as Toreador; the proper word is Torero, the bull-man. The score of *Carmen* has wonderful Spanish rhythms and melodious arias, which appeal to the average opera-goer and to professional musicians as well.

Grand opera has its younger and gayer relative—the operetta, which literally means little opera. Operettas often make fun of their respectable relative. The amusing operettas of Gilbert and Sullivan are wonderful caricatures of Italian operas—and their arias are almost as beautiful as Verdi's. Here all the nonsense of operatic stage action is converted into hilarious horseplay. A chorus of policemen sings for five minutes, *On the foe do we go,* without budging, until the heroine reminds them that they are not going anywhere. A ship captain is exchanged as a baby with a sailor. A boy is apprenticed by mistake as a pirate (instead of a pilot, because his nurse was hard of hearing) until his twenty-first birthday. He was born on February 29, and his twenty-first birthday would not come until the age of eighty-four, and that would be 1940, according to the libretto. The date, 1940, of course sounded impossibly distant at the time the operetta was written, and it ought now to be changed to 2040, in order to avoid an anti-climax.

In old Vienna, by the Blue Danube, operettas are even more popular than grand operas. Johann Strauss, the Waltz King, wrote witty operettas, and in modern times, Franz Lehar revived the art of old Vienna. His operetta, *The Merry Widow,* is a perennial on the stage all over the world.

In France, too, operettas found a fertile field. The gay Parisian, Jacques Offenbach, specialized on making fun of Greek mythology. Dancing to his rhythmic music, the Greek war leaders are quite undignified on the stage, while Helen of Troy chatters as engagingly as any Parisian midinette.

If opera is the child of Italy, ballet is the offspring of France. In the opera, all terms are Italian. In ballet, everything is French. The word ballet itself is French, meaning a little ball. Then, there are the Arabesque and the Pirouette and the Entrechat and the Pas de Deux. But the name for a leading dancer is Italian, ballerina.

The subjects for these ballets were usually taken from classical literature, with cupids and zephyrs, muses and fauns disporting themselves on the stage. In the days when France had a king, the imperial palace was often converted into a stage, and the ballet was turned into a masked ball.

At first, ballet served as a display of graceful motion and exquisite costume. But under the influence of opera and drama, the French ballet developed its own stage action, and a complete story in dance was unfolded before the spectator. In one ballet, the central figure is an automatic doll, who has to be wound up each morning. When she gets unwound, the music slows up in a very realistic way. She attracts the attention of a moonstruck suitor, whose disappointment after the discovery that she is merely a doll is very acute.

The Russians developed such an extraordinary technique of classical toe-dancing that Russian ballerinas outdid even the original creators of ballet dancing, the French. There was Pavlova, whose dance of the dying swan fascinated the world. There was Nijinsky, who could leap from the stage through an open window into the wings as if gravity did not exist. So successful are Russian ballet dancers, that ballerinas of other lands often assume Russian names. There are several famous ballerinas whose stage names have the ending *ova,* but who are really Miss Smith or Jones.

By the Courtesy of the Gramophone Co., Ltd.

CARICATURE OF CARUSO MAKING A RECORD

Drawn by himself

✂23✂

Musical Geography

THE best known melodies are composed by men and women who know nothing about the theory of composition. The chances are that folk music is a collective creation. A villager sings a song while working in the field; another singer picks it up, unconsciously making changes in the words and the tune, and soon the entire village sings it. Then some musician from town hears the song and writes it down, making further changes in the original.

The keepers of folksong traditions are old men and women whose memories are strong, and whose lives are quiet and undisturbed by the hubbub of modern life. The ancient melody of the Inca Indians, the *Hymn to the Sun,* was preserved by a 117-year-old Peruvian Indian. A musician, who heard the Indian, gives a vivid description of the way he sang: "Despite his advanced age, the muscular body of this Indian enabled him to walk erect with the martial gait of a soldier. Indians, as a race, are reserved and uncommunicative. But when the spirit moves them, they grow eloquent. One day he invited me to go hunting. Later, having regaled me with a splendid heron he had shot that morning, he said to me: 'You will now hear the hymn we sing to the Sun.' And he intoned this mystical chant, saved from oblivion in the silent memory of an ancient Indian."

INCA HYMN TO THE SUN

Musical education is actually harmful to folk singing. There is a story of a young girl from South Carolina who had a natural talent for singing Southern ballads. She became quite a celebrity in her home town, and the local Chamber of Commerce decided to send her to Europe to study. When she came back several years later, she could sing German classics but she had forgotten her native ballads. Folk singing was "cultured out" of her.

One of the greatest folk songs is the *Londonderry Air,* collected in northern Ireland. It was published not quite a hundred years ago, in an album of Irish songs, and the composer's name was unknown. Yet musicians of our day, with all their education and knowledge, cannot write a melody to match the perfect symmetry and melodic balance of this anonymous air.

In Russia, the *Song of the Volga Boatmen* expresses in its slow swaying rhythms all the sadness of the Russian people. This song was sung for centuries by the workers who dragged boats upstream with a rope looped around their bodies.

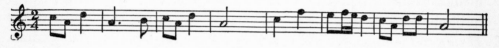

THE SONG OF THE VOLGA BOATMEN

In America, cowbody songs of the West, and Negro spirituals of the South reveal the inner life of the people. The history, the geography, and the folklore of America are reflected in these songs and ballads more faithfully than they are in any textbooks and anthologies.

In rare cases, identifiable composers have written melodies that have become folk songs. Stephen Foster, the author of *Old Folks at Home, Oh, Susanna,* and many other popular songs, is a true folksong composer. *Dixie* was also a composed song, and its author was Dan Emmett. One of the best known Latin-American folksongs, *Estrellita,* was composed by a Mexican musician, Manuel Ponce.

Popular dance music, too, belongs to national folklore. Nobody knows who invented the square dances of America, the Morris dances in England, the Russian Cossack dances, the Italian Tarantella, the Spanish Fandango, the Irish Jig, the Scottish Reel, or the Cuban Rumba. These dances are as natural as language and song.

The art of folk song is alive even in modern times. Music scholars everywhere are busy collecting these simple melodies that are so strangely beautiful and so unmistakably genuine. One does not have to go far in search of this treasure of folk music. Often a next door neighbor has a large repertoire of native songs, even though he is not aware of their origin.

In the cities, too, there are folk songs in factories and even in business offices. There are songs of street peddlers, fishmongers, knife grinders, and ragmen. The French composer, Charpentier, incorporated the cries of Paris street vendors in his opera, *Louise*. The counterpoint of fish and fruit makes a wonderful chorus.

In the new mechanical civilization, the singing commercials of the radio are the street cries of today. They possess a strange fascination that overcomes and disarms. It is entirely possible that Pepsi-Cola Hits the Spot or the little ditty about the banana that comes from the very tropical equator and should not be put in the refrigerator will become the folk tunes of tomorrow.

❧ 24 ❧

Greece, the Cradle of Music

THE musical words of the opera stage are Italian, and of the ballet, French. But the basic musical terms are Greek, for Greece was the cradle of organized music. Music . . . why, the word Music is Greek. It is the art of the Muses. Also Greek are the words Tone, Chord, Melody, Harmony, Rhythm, Orchestra, Organ, Rhapsody, Fantasia, Chorus, and even Harmonica.

The word Lyre is Greek, too, as is the word lyrical, and lyrics, which is a rather lowbrow term for the words of popular songs. The lyre is the instrument of Apollo. Orpheus, the son of Apollo and the Muse Calliope (she gave the name to a less poetic instrument, the calliope of the amusement park), played the lyre so enchantingly that he could soothe the savage breasts of gods and humans with the charm of his music. When his bride wandered away into the region of Pluto, Orpheus sang to the accompaniment of his lyre so persuasively that Tantalus stopped trying to get a drink of water, Sisyphus ceased to roll rocks uphill, and the Furies themselves shed sentimental tears.

The lyre is the very symbol of music. It is represented in classical paintings; it adorns the title page of every published composition, and the portal of every music school. The backs of chairs are sometimes designed like a lyre. The lyre is the only musical instrument that gave the name to a living creature—the lyrebird of Australia, whose tail feathers spread in the form of the lyre. The lyrebird has a good singing voice of mellow tone, and possesses an extraordinary talent for imitating the calls of other Australian birds.

There is an expression "to run the gamut of emotion." The word Gamut comes from the Greek letter Gamma, or our G, which was the lowest note of the Greek scale system.

So, from lyrics to chorus, from a symphony orchestra to the calliope, the inhabitants of the world of music are heirs to ancient Greek culture. Yet, there is nothing tangible left of Greek music. A few skeletons of lyres can be seen in museums, but they hardly give any idea of the charm of the lyres in Greek mythology. No one knows what the lyre really sounded like. Perhaps it is just as well. After the modern piano and the violin, the lyre with its thin sound might make us wonder why it was the favorite instrument of the Greek gods.

AUSTRALIAN LYRE BIRD

The first concerts of music were given in Greece twenty-seven centuries ago, during the Olympic games, at which flutists and trumpeters were the main attractions. They were amply rewarded. At the Olympic games in Athens, in the year 776 B.C., a flute player brought in as a certificate of his professional standing the picture of a stone column erected in his honor by the grateful audiences at his previous appearance. Then a trumpeter played a solo on a six-foot trumpet.

The ancient Greeks were the first to arrange the scale in diatonic degrees. The word Diatonic is Greek, too, and it means "coming through the tone." Also Greek is the word Chromatic, from Chromos, color. The musical modes, Ionian, Dorian, Phrygian, Lydian, Mixolydian, Aeolian, and Locrian, are all named after various provinces and districts of ancient Greece. Each mode reflected a personal characteristic, according to Greek philosophers of Plato's school. Some modes were regarded as vigorous and manly, others mild or serene. Apparently, the Greeks were more sensitive to the nature of intervals than we are now. In our music, we are left with only two scales, major and minor, and the modes are so strange to our ears that they are, well, just Greek to us! In addition to these diatonic modes, the Greeks had a scale with quarter-tones, and the lyre was tuned to produce these minute intervals.

Although we have inherited the names of musical modes from Greece, these names do not coincide with the original Greek modes, because the Greeks counted their intervals downwards. This mixup occurred because the Greek high notes are our low notes, and our low notes are their high notes. In naming their notes by the length of the string, the Greeks were more logical, because long strings are higher when stood up vertically, and short strings lower. Accordingly, when the Greeks spoke of manly high notes, they were notes produced by the long strings of the lyre, and long strings make bass-like sounds. A little reflection can straighten it out in our minds.

The Greeks had a musical notation, too, not with lines and notes, but with Greek letters turned sideways, or upside down. This notation indicated what lyre string was to be played, much as our popular composers show the position of the ukelele strings for those who cannot read music. Here is an invisible thread connecting ancient Greece with Broadway.

໑25໑

Monks and Minstrels

THE glory of Greece gave way to the grandeur of Rome. The art of music shifted to Italy. The greatest advance in musical theory was made one thousand years ago when an Italian monk named Guido, from the town of Arezzo, established a method of teaching music and named the notes of the scale with the syllables of a Latin hymn. The melody of this hymn happened to be arranged in such a way that the first verse began with the first note of the scale, the second verse with the second, and so forth up to the sixth line. These syllables were Ut, Re, Mi, Fa, Sol, and La. Ut was difficult to sing and was changed later to Do. Re was the beginning of a Latin word related to Resonance; Mi was for Miracle; Fa for Family, Sol for Solve, and La for Labial, pertaining to lips. Guido's scales had only six notes, and it was considerably later that the seventh note was added, Si, made up of the initials for Saint John.

After the naming of the notes, it became necessary to invent some kind of understandable musical notation. In Guido's time, the only possible way of writing musical notes was by accents. The acute accent, as in the French word *passé,* meant a high note; the grave accent, as in the French word, *père,* stood for a low note. But there was no way of indicating the exact interval between the low and the high note. Some anonymous genius of a scribe took the next step by drawing a horizontal line across the manuscript, and disposing his accents higher or lower according to the approximate interval from the note on the line. Soon copyists of musical manuscripts found that one line was not enough, and they drew a second line for another note. These two lines were in different colors, yellow and red, and there was a letter at the beginning of each line indicating the exact note of the line. For instance, the upper line would be marked C, and the lower F. Notes between F and C would be put on the spaces between the lines, according to intervals. These letters developed into our familiar clefs.

Credit for the development of musical notes, lines, and clefs belongs to the monks in European monasteries. More lines were drawn for a more accurate representation of musical intervals. One English monk invented a staff of eleven lines, but this system was too cumbersome to succeed. For three centuries after Guido of Arezzo, the most common system was a music staff of four lines. It was only much later that the fifth line was added.

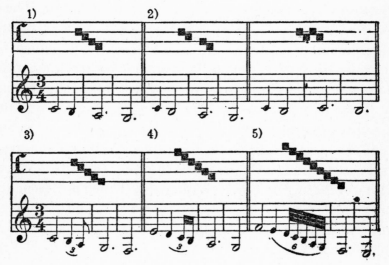

THE MUSICAL ALPHABET OF 500 YEARS AGO

In the meantime, musical notes underwent several transformations. From accents they developed into wriggles, then clusters of dots, and then separate notes, diamond-shaped, oblong, and square. The square note persisted for several centuries before giving way to our familiar circular notes. In some ways, the old notation was superior. By means of a cluster of squares, the composer could represent the whole melody, with the duration and position clearly indicated. There were no bar lines, but the division of phrases was shown in a very ingenious manner. Musical sentences are often chopped up in our notation by the bar lines, while in old music writing, a musical phrase stood out by itself, and could be shaped with more understanding. Nowadays, music students who have no intelligent interest in what they play, put an accent on every first beat of the bar, regardless of the musical phrase which overlaps the bar lines. This habit contributes a great deal to the un-musical pounding of beginners. Imagine how much better it would be if there were no bar lines, but groups of musical phrases indicated by a cluster of notes of different shapes and colors!

It was thirteen centuries ago that Pope Gregory established the first rules for religious singing. These rules are embodied in the system of church music that is known as Gregorian Chant—or Plain Chant, because the singing line was unaccompanied. It was seven centuries ago that Plain Chant was supplemented by new methods of musical composition which became known as The New Art. Church music was vocal music, without instrumental accompaniment, and the language of the text was Latin.

But outside the churches and monasteries, a new type of music began to develop. It was the music of the people sung in the language of the people, in French, in Italian, in Spanish. Sometimes, a Latin church song was taken as a theme, and variations were interwoven about that theme, in different languages. This type of musical melting pot became known as a Quodlibet, which means the same as Ad libitum, at will. Even the great Bach was fascinated by the Quodlibet type of composition, and in his Goldberg Variations combined two popular songs, *Long Have I Been Away* and *Cabbage and Turnips,* in an intricate counterpuntal web.

The first popular song in the English language was a canon composed by an unknown Englishman seven centuries ago to celebrate the coming of summer, *"Sumer is icumen in, loudly sings Cuckoo."* The manuscript of this canon is preserved in the British Museum. It is written with square black notes, on the music staff of six lines, and the lines are traced in red. This song was well in advance of the harmony and counterpoint of church singing, and is therefore regarded as of great historical importance.

Church singing did not remain on the unison basis for a long time. The boys, whose voices were high, sang a fifth above the tenors, and the melody went on in consecutive fifths—the very thing that is forbidden in classical harmony. This singing in consecutive fifths was the rule until the advent of the New Art, seven centuries ago, when thirds and sixths were first introduced into choral singing. Consecutive thirds and sixths are, of course, the very foundation of classical music, but these intervals were regarded as dissonant by the medieval scholars, and there was as much opposition to this New Art on the part of their conservative contemporaries as there is now to modern dissonant music.

Rhythm, too, began to come into its own. A distinction was made between perfect and imperfect time. Perfect time had three beats to a bar, and was indicated by a circle, as a symbol of roundness, completeness, and perfection. Imperfect time was marked by a semicircle to show that it is unfinished, cut off, imperfect. Our time signature for 4/4 time is a relic of this semicircle. It looks like a letter C, and some people, even professional musicians, believe that this C stands for Common time, but it is absolutely wrong. In this case, C is not a letter, but a half of a circle.

While learned monks industriously copied music on parchment, another kind of music, the music of the people, was spread by popular entertainers, minstrels and troubadours. Like radio singers of today, the troubadours could not read music, and did not know the notes. But they possessed a natural feeling for melody. Some of the minstrel songs became so widely known that even learned musicians took them up, and wrote counterpoint around them. One such song was a French popular ditty about a soldier, *L'Homme Armé*. Several composers of music used this song as a theme for contrapuntal works, and even introduced it into religious scores.

The Armed Man, A MEDIEVAL HIT TUNE

Minstrels and troubadours must have been very versatile, to judge by an account in an old German chronicle. It says that musical entertainers were able "to play the drum, the cymbal, and the hurdy-gurdy; to throw small apples, and to catch knives; to perform card tricks, and

to jump through hoops." How many educated musicians could qualify
for such a job nowadays?

A TRAVELING MINSTREL

26

The Dawn of Classical Music

FEW musicians realize that up to five hundred years ago, composers wrote only vocal music. Instruments merely doubled the vocal parts, without contributing anything new in harmony and counterpoint. Old musical scores were often marked: "to be sung or played on instruments." It was not necessary to specify what particular instruments were to be used, because instrumental parts were written within a limited range, not more than two octaves, and any instrument could play the music. Our violins, clarinets, and pianos did not yet exist. Yet beautiful music was played on lutes, recorders, and spinets. The lute resembled a guitar with its neck bent backwards. The spinet was the grandmother of our piano—grandmother, not grandfather, because only ladies played on spinets. The recorder was a vertical flute, popular in Shakespeare's time. Pepys, the famous author of a seventeenth century diary, liked to play on the recorder for recreation. Later, the recorder disappeared from circulation until an enterprising English instrument-maker, Dolmetsch, revived the instrument for modern use. It was a most successful revival, and recorders have regained their popularity, particularly among young folks.

Instrumental music was still in its infancy when vocal compositions were written by the greatest composers of the age. In the fifteenth and sixteenth centuries, vocal music of a highly complex nature flourished in Holland and Belgium. This was the period known in music history as polyphonic. The word, poly, means many; the second part of the word polyphonic is the same as in phone and phonograph, meaning sound. So polyphonic music is a type of composition that combines many themes in multiple counterpoint. In polyphonic music, each part is an independent melody, and these independent melodies combine to create an effect that is harmonious and pleasing to the ear.

Polyphonic music, written exclusively for voices without instruments, is extremely difficult to perform. The singers must be thorough musicians in order to bring out the proper balance of a polyphonic ensemble, and they must keep perfect pitch throughout the performance. Nowadays, when specialization in music separates composer

A VERSATILE MUSICIAN
AS PICTURED IN AN OLD CARTOON

from singer, and singer from instrumentalist, it is difficult to find such trained musicians as existed four centuries ago when singers and performers had to be composers and arrangers as well.

A few names of the great school of Holland and Belgium (this school is known as Flemish) should be remembered, even though they never appear on symphony programs, or on the radio. They are Oke-ghem, Josquin des Près, and Orlando di Lasso. But these Flemish musicians did not have a monopoly on polyphonic music. In Italy there was the great Palestrina, who was a contemporary of Orlando di Lasso. In fact, the two died in the same year, 1594, only a few months apart.

While the Flemish composers emphasized the ingenuity of counter-point, Palestrina wrote in a harmonic style, thinking of chords and progressions rather than combinations of independent voices. For this reason, Palestrina's music is easier to perform, and is closer to our own idea of harmony. Palestrina is important in music history because he wrote church music in a style much more ingratiating than the auster-ity and detachment of the Gregorian Chant.

The age of Palestrina and the Flemish masters marked the dawn of classical music. No longer did composers regard instruments as an un-important background for singing voices. The development of the church organ as a solo instrument led to the composition of intricate works for the organ. In Italy, the family of great violin makers, Stradi-varius, manufactured string instruments of amazing tonal beauty. Even modern science, that can anlayze the chemical composition of the wood and the varnish of a Stradivarius violin, is unable to repro-duce an instrument remotely approaching the almost human warmth that distinguishes these old masterpieces. And it is a thrill to every musician to look into the ∫-shaped holes of an old Italian violin and read the inscription in Latin: *Stradivarius fecit A.D. 1720.*

The manufacture of violins by Stradivarius and his contemporaries helped the development of the violin as a solo instrument. Soon violin-like instruments began to be manufactured in different sizes—the viola, the violoncello, and the double bass. There were other string instruments, such as viola d' amore (the violin of love) and the viola da gamba (the knee viola, held between the knees). Groups of string instruments formed small orchestras. During the reign of Louis XIV in France, the Italian-born master, Lully, conducted a violin orches-tra, known as Les Petits Violons du Roi. He conducted so vigorously that during one of his concerts he struck his toe with his long, sharp-pointed conducting baton. His foot became infected. That was long before penicillin and other wonder drugs, and Lully's infection proved fatal. He died a victim of his musical temperament.

At the time Stradivarius was making his violins, another Italian instrument maker, Cristofori, developed a keyboard instrument which he named the Pianoforte, because it could play *piano* (soft) and *forte* (loud). The immediate predecessors of the piano were the Harpsichord and the Clavichord but they could play only *piano,* or rather *tintinnando,* which means tinkling. One of the original Cristofori pianos is now in the Metropolitan Museum of Art in New York. Ironically enough, we never call the pianoforte by its full name, but abbreviate it to Piano, which is definitely an injustice to those who can pound the *piano* very, very *forte.*

～27～

The Giants of Music

BY THE year 1700, music had reached its maturity. The musical alphabet was complete. There were excellent musical tools, string instruments, keyboard instruments, wood-winds and brasses. The stage was set for masters of the art to create with these tools a new kind of music, in which melody, harmony, rhythm, and instrumental color would blend in a perfect bouquet. All that was necessary was a skillful combination of these elements, and—genius.

Musical geniuses did appear, and classical music as we know it became a historical fact. What names! Johann Sebastian Bach. Wolfgang Amadeus Mozart. George Frederick Handel. Franz Josef Haydn. Ludwig van Beethoven.

The word Bach means a stream in German, and indeed Bach is the fountainhead of classical music. He is the founder of musical science. No wonder modern musicians are devoted admirers of Bach, for Bach's music is a triumph of technique, as well as an inspired revelation of genius. Before Bach, composers did not dare to write more than two or three sharps or flats in the key signature, because the tuning was not standardized, and the chromatic scale was not divided into equal semitones. As a result, a melody played on black keys sounded out of tune. Bach proposed to establish a democracy in tonal relationships, so that all semitones would be equal, with or without black keys.

As a manual for this new musical democracy, he wrote two volumes of fugues and preludes in all major and minor keys. He called this collection *The Well-Tempered Clavichord*. The words well-tempered in the title mean that all intervals are equalized, tempered well, like steel in a forge, and made smooth and hard.

Bach was born in the year 1685. Bach's father and Bach's uncle were identical twins. They looked so much alike that their own wives could not tell them apart, recognizing them only by the different clothing they wore. One is tempted to ask, would Bach have been a great musician if he had been his uncle's son.

Bach was a fine organist, and it was as an organ player in German churches that he earned his living. His great compositions were to him part of a job, since he had to provide hymns and chorales for the congregation. When he employed too much counterpoint in his organ playing, his church superiors called him to account. The parishioners could not follow the tune through the web of intricate variations, Bach was told, and would he kindly desist from this practice? He obliged, and kept his more difficult compositions out of hearing.

Bach was married twice and had twenty children, including a pair of twins. Ten of his children died in infancy, and of the remaining ten, three achieved great prominence as musicians and composers. The last of Bach's direct descendants died a hundred years ago, but there are musicians living now who bear the proud name of Bach. They are the progeny of Bach's distant relatives.

Bach lived quietly as a respected musician, but few contemporaries were aware of his gigantic magnitude in music history. Handel, who was born only a short distance from Bach's birthplace in central Germany, and within a few weeks of Bach's birth, never met Bach. He was socially more successful than his great contemporary. He wrote music that was more easily understood by the people—operas, oratorios, and suites. In pursuit of greater opportunities, Handel went to London, and became a favorite composer in England. He anglicized his name by eliminating the two dots over the letter "a" in the German original Händel, and called himself George Frideric, in the mistaken belief that Frideric was the proper English spelling of his German name, Friedrich. When King George I arranged a festival on the River Thames, Handel composed special music for the occasion, known as Water Music. When George II became king, he, too, bestowed bounties and commissions on Handel. For him, Handel wrote the Royal Fireworks music which was performed at the celebration of the peace treaty between France and England. Cannon shots were fired before the presentation of the music; then when fireworks were set off they started a small conflagration, which spoiled somewhat the success of the festivities.

Great as was Handel, he had a rival in the affections of British music lovers—an Italian composer whose name is utterly insignificant in comparison with that of Handel. He was Buononcini, a composer of operas and oratorios, who went to London about the same time as Handel. This rivalry became quite a topic of discussion in English society, and a verse was published in a London paper commenting upon it.

> Some say, compared to Buononcini
> That Mein Herr Handel's but a ninny;
> Others aver that he to Handel
> Is scarcely fit to hold a candle.
> Strange all this difference should be
> Twixt tweedledum and tweedledee.

Incidentally, this was the first time that tweedledum and tweedledee appeared in the English language, and so Handel unwittingly contributed to the vocabulary of his adopted country.

Handel's most celebrated work is his oratorio, *The Messiah,* which he composed in three weeks. Shortly after he conducted it in London, he began to lose his eyesight. A surgeon performed a cataract operation, but it was a failure. By strange coincidence, Bach, too, lost his eyesight in the years before his death, and the same surgeon performed an operation on Bach's eye. The methods were crude: the doctor cut out the lens and let it drop to the bottom of the eyeball. Bach's operation, too, was unsuccessful. Bach died in 1750 and was buried in a little German town; a notice appeared in the local paper announcing the death of a well-known musician. Handel died in London nine years later, and was buried with great honors in Westminster Abbey.

Handel's name is frequently associated with Haydn, although Haydn belonged to a later generation. But both Haydn and Handel wrote oratorios, and both possessed dignity and spiritual power. Furthermore, Handel and Haydn are hyphenated in numerous Handel and Haydn societies, dedicated to performances of works by the two great H's of music.

Haydn, too, lived in London, but he did not remain in England, did not write music for English kings, and was not buried in Westminster Abbey. Haydn is usually called the father of the symphony. As a matter of fact, the first real symphony was composed by a little-known musician named Stamitz, some two hundred years ago. But Haydn was the first to write symphonies in mass production. Many of these symphonies are known by nicknames: the *Surprise Symphony,* which has a big drum crash (there is a story that Haydn put this loud drum in to wake up London ladies who were in the habit of dozing off during the concert); the *Clock Symphony,* which had the imitation of a tick-tock beat, and even a *Philosopher Symphony.* Then there was the *Toy Symphony* for children, with a toy trumpet, a rattle, and a cuckoo whistle in the score. The wittiest of Haydn's symphonies was the *Farewell Symphony,* in which musicians were instructed to leave one after another towards the end of the last movement until a solitary violin remained all by its lonely self. The violinist was supposed to blow out the candles when he finished the last note.

According to the accepted count, there are one hundred and four Haydn symphonies, but a few dozen more which he probably never wrote were published under Haydn's name. Music publishers in those days had little compunction about capitalizing on a great name. When a successful composer died, they commissioned a competent musician to write more music by the departed composer. To this day music scholars cannot decide which Haydn symphonies were written during his lifetime and which ones were ghost productions. This is, of course, a great tribute to the ghost composers. They must have been proficient enough to provide a good imitation of the dead master's music.

Bach, Handel and Haydn lived long lives and gave to the world the full fruits of their labors. Mozart lived only one-half of the Biblical threescore and ten years. He was born twenty-four years after Haydn; yet Haydn outlived him by seventeen and a half years.

Mozart had a prodigious facility in composition, and could write an orchestral work in one afternoon. During the thirty-five years, ten months and nine days of his life, Mozart wrote so much music that a German scholar, Ludwig von Koechel, who lived seventy-seven years, five months, and nineteen days, devoted his entire life to the job of cataloguing Mozart's compositions, without completing his task,

Mozart was the most phenomenal child prodigy in music history. His father, who was an excellent musician, trained Mozart in a businesslike manner, with a view to lucrative appearances as a performer on the clavichord. Mozart played for the royalty of European capitals, and the family received generous remuneration. Unfortunately, when Mozart grew up and became a mere genius of a composer, his social success faded. He had to endure poverty and want. Often he was reduced to writing begging letters to a friend who was a banker. One of these letters was recently sold at an auction in New York for six hundred dollars. Poor Mozart! If only he had known that all he had to do to raise money was to write a begging letter and then wait a century and a half to sell the autograph for many times the amount asked in the letter!

The secret of Mozart's genius is not easy to describe. One speaks of Mozart's simplicity and charm, his prodigious melodic invention, his perfection and symmetry of form, his transparency of harmonic texture. Mozart's music is gay and light in the compositions in major keys and fast tempos. But he could also be profound and philosophical when he wrote a slow movement in a minor key. Mozart did not cultivate learned music, and his vocabulary of chords and harmonic progressions is amazingly simple. But with these unassuming musical means Mozart succeeded in creating more variety than a composer using a whole arsenal of ingenious devices.

Mozart's last work was a Mass for the Dead, a Requiem, which happened to be written under dramatic circumstances. One day a stranger, clad in black, appeared at Mozart's door and asked him if he would be willing to compose a requiem for him. Mozart agreed, but before he could finish the task, he fell ill of typhoid fever. In his delirium he remembered the stranger. Who could he be? Was he a messenger of death, who had diabolically commissioned Mozart's own Requiem? The mystery was not cleared up until many years after Mozart's death. The stranger was the man servant of a wealthy citizen, who intended to have the Requiem performed as his own work and had veiled his communications with Mozart in secrecy to shield his identity.

Lovable and cheerful as Mozart was in life, he, too, possessed envious rivals. One of these rivals was the Italian musician, Salieri. After Mozart's death, a legend grew that Salieri had poisoned him, a legend perpetuated in an opera by Rimsky-Korsakov, entitled *Mozart and Salieri*. In it, Salieri bemoans the fact that Mozart could create music of heavenly beauty without effort, while he, Salieri, who slaved all his life to master the science of musical tones, produced but mediocre pieces. "Then fly to the celestial regions, whence you came!" exclaims Salieri, and slips poison into Mozart's cup.

The last of the giants of the classical era was Beethoven. His early compositions possessed Mozart-like charm, but in the middle of his life there appeared in his music a stormy element unlike anything heard before. With titanic strength, Beethoven broke the chains of classical harmony. His music assumed a brooding quality, full of drama. There were strange outbursts of passionate arpeggios and ca-denzas. His piano sonatas steered farther and farther away from the classical formula. And in his Ninth Symphony he wrote a chord com-bining all the seven steps of the D Minor scale, which was, of course, a defiance of musical tradition.

Beethoven's life was marked with the most tragic misfortune that can befall a musician. When still a young man, he began to lose his hearing. He had to converse in writing, using a notebook. Conducting his own symphonies, he could not hear what the orchestra was playing. Some of his critics explained the strangeness of his music by the fact that he could not hear it. They did not understand that this strangeness was the sign of a new era in which music became intensely human, the era of ro-mantic art. Classical music was exquisite. It soothed the senses and gave the listener a feeling of satisfaction and contentment. But the new music that Beethoven wrote was stirring and disquieting. Despite his deafness, Beethoven could precipitate oceans of sound, and unleash avalanches of power that did not lose their grandeur for succeeding generations of musicians. The four notes of the theme of the *Fifth Symphony* are a clarion call of humanity, understandable to all peo-ples in the world. And his *Heroic Symphony*—usually known under its Italian name, *Eroica*—still retains the revolutionary meaning that Beethoven gave it. The story of its dedication to Napoleon is well known. When Napoleon proclaimed himself Emperor, Beethoven crossed out his dedication and wrote instead, "To the Memory of a Great Man." It is not true, as is often told, that Beethoven tore up the title page. The original manuscript of the Symphony is still preserved, and the title page is intact, only Napoleon's name is carefully crossed out in black ink.

Beethoven's end came when he was not yet old—only fifty-six. A flash of lightning and a deafening clap of thunder accompanied his last moments, as though nature itself addressed him in dramatic, Beethoven-like tones.

28

Romantic Composers

BACH, Handel, Haydn, Mozart, Beethoven, were German or Austrian musicians—an amazing concentration of great men in a small area of Europe! Vienna became the music capital early in the nineteenth century—Beethoven, Haydn, Schubert, and later Brahms lived there. The history of humanity teaches us that peoples and nations are seldom aware of the presence of great men among them. Sometimes these great men are respected and noticed in the press, but they are allowed to languish in poverty, for the products of their genius are rarely marketable. Beethoven was in constant need of money, as was Mozart before him. But they at least enjoyed world-wide recognition in their lifetime. Schubert, who died at thirty-one, did not live long enough to realize that he was a great musician. He never met Beethoven, though he lived in the same city with him.

When Schubert died, his personal effects, including a large number of manuscripts, were sold for the equivalent of a few dollars. Fortunately, the manuscripts fell into friendly hands, and were preserved. One by one, in the course of years, Schubert's songs, his piano pieces, his overtures and, finally, his symphonies, were published. Songs that Schubert wrote at the age of seventeen are now acknowledged as among the greatest ever written. His symphonies are equal in rank to Mozart's and Beethoven's. But although Schubert left an enormous amount of finished compositions, his most celebrated work is the *Unfinished Symphony*. Of course, Schubert did not call it the Unfinished Symphony, and the reasons why he left it unfinished are not clear. He composed it at the age of twenty-six, when he had still five years to live. Yet he sent it to a musical society with only two movements completed and a few bars of the third movement in sketch form.

In the romantic era, the personalities of the composers became almost as important as their music. The great classicists were content with writing music for music's sake. Romantic composers were brought up in the belief that they were fighters for a cause, the spearhead of fresh young forces against reaction. Their weapon was music. One of these fighting romantics was Robert Schumann. He even started an imaginary Society of David with the purpose of combating the Philistines of the arts. He divided his personality into several parts, and called them by symbolic names, such as Eusebius, or Florestan, expressive of different sides of his nature.

The story of Schumann's romantic love for Clara, the daughter of his teacher, is a moving episode. Although Schumann's teacher recognized his musical abilities, he did not think of Schumann as a desirable son-in-law in a practical world. He opposed the growing friendship between his daughter and the young composer, even resorting to legal means of preventing their marriage. They did marry nevertheless, and their union was one of the happiest in the history of romantic love. Clara Schumann was a remarkable pianist. She was better known to the general public than Schumann himself, who was often referred to as the husband of the great Clara. He did not resent it, although he had tried to become a virtuoso pianist himself. He practiced hard, too hard, and in the ambitious determination to improve his technique, he tied a string to the naturally weak fourth finger and kept pulling the string for exercise until the muscles became permanently injured.

Clara's success as a pianist and Schumann's success as a composer made it possible for them and their children to live without concern about the necessities of life. Then came tragedy. Schumann was stricken with an inexplicable mental illness. He could not work. He imagined he heard someone constantly tuning middle A on an invisible instrument. He became absorbed in his inner visions. One day he went to the bank of the Rhine, and jumped into its chilly waters. When he was rescued he himself asked to be sent to a sanitarium to be isolated from the world. There he died. Clara Schumann survived him for many years, and there are still people living who knew her as the great old lady of music.

Schumann's friend and contemporary, Felix Mendelssohn, was born under the luckiest star that ever shone upon a musician. His life was short, but unclouded by struggle or tragedy. The very name, Felix, the happy one, was prophetic. He was the son of a banker, and the only

great composer in music history who had the private means to give
him security and peace of mind. His family was musical; there were
concerts in Mendelssohn's home, and at a very early age Mendelssohn
was introduced to classical music. Also while very young he began to
compose. His musical career was marked by an immediate success. He
was the darling of Queen Victoria, for whom he often played during
his visits to London. And it was in England that Mendelssohn's *Wedding March* was performed for the first time, on the occasion of the
marriage of the Princess Royal, in 1858.

Like Mozart and Schubert, Mendelssohn possessed an inexhaustible
facility in musical production. Symphonies, oratorios, concertos,
piano pieces, and songs came off his pen with incredible ease. Still
unpublished are numerous compositions of Mendelssohn, including
five operas which he wrote as a young boy.

And then came Brahms. With his long professorial beard, Brahms
did not look like a romantic composer. His life was devoid of colorful episodes. He never married, and his one relaxation was to sit at
the table of a sidewalk café in Vienna and listen to gypsy dances played
by a Hungarian orchestra. He was not precocious, and did not
write his first symphony until he was past forty. His friend, the German conductor, Hans von Buelow, called him the third B of the
three great B's of music, Bach, Beethoven and Brahms, and this witty
saying established Brahms as an immediate successor of Beethoven.
Beethoven was born twenty years after Bach's death. Brahms was born
six years after Beethoven's death, so that there is a close chronological
progression.

As a matter of fact, von Buelow put it this way: "My musical faith
is in E Flat Major, with three flats in the key signature: Bach, Beethoven and Brahms." In the German musical scale B is our B Flat.
Buelow used the letter B, by extension, for the other two flats of E Flat
Major as well.

To this, a friend who heard von Buelow's remark, observed: "You
might add an H, so as to modulate into the relative minor key." This
kind of humor is rather complicated, and requires explanation. The
H stands for Handel, and H is also the German letter-note for our B
natural. The simplest way of modulating from E Flat Major, with
Bach, Beethoven and Brahms in the key signature, into its relative

minor key, which is C Minor, is by leading B Flat chromatically to B Natural, and B natural is the German H for Handel!

MUSIC'S THREE B'S AND AN H

Classical composers confined their inspiration to the realm of absolute music, which had little contact with the natural music and popular songs of their own lands. Romantic composers, responsive to the appeal of the soil, wrote music in a national style, with folk rhythms and melodies.

Carl Maria von Weber, a contemporary of Beethoven, was the first German composer who used native folklore as a basis of his music. His romantic operas reflect the original spirit of the people, just as the German fairy tales reflect the poetry of the nation.

Composers of other nations followed Weber's lead, and wrote music in the national style, based on popular folklore. Dvořák and Smetana, in Bohemia, immortalized the folkways of the Czech people in their operas and symphonies. Grieg acquainted the world with the fascinating tales of Norway, the creatures of the mountains and the rustic gayety of the Norwegian countryside. In Finland, the great Sibelius has pictured in his symphonic poems the epical lore of his northern land.

England, for a long time the host to famous Germans—Handel, Haydn, Mendelssohn—contributed to the new spirit of musical nationalism, in the majestic and martial music of Sir Edward Elgar (whose march, *Pomp and Circumstance,* is famous the world over) and in the poetic art of Ralph Vaughan Williams, the author of a *London Symphony,* in which the street noises of the British capital are integrated into a symphonic form.

The most amazing flowering of romantic nationalism in music took place in Russia. The first Russian composer who set Russian subjects to music was Glinka, a contemporary of Schumann and Mendelssohn. The word Glinka in Russian means "little clay." After the production of Glinka's opera *A Life for the Czar,* the Russian poet Pushkin (whose name means cannon, and not pushing) greeted him in verse, saying that Glinka was no longer "little clay," but precious porcelain.

Russian composers who followed Glinka continued to use native elements in their symphonic and instrumental compositions. Particularly militant in this respect was a group of composers known as the Mighty Five. As a matter of fact, only three of them were really mighty in the sense that their music was powerful and important, Borodin, Moussorgsky and Rimsky-Korsakov. The remaining two of the Mighty Five, Balakirev and Cui, did not leave works of lasting value, and are little more than names in music history books.

The interesting circumstance about the Mighty Five is that music was for them only an avocation, a hobby rather than the principal profession. Thus Borodin began his career as a medical student and became professor of chemistry in a girls' college. To the end of his life, he regarded himself as a chemist rather than a musician, and composed relatively little. But all that he wrote is of enduring value to Russian music. His opera *Prince Igor,* written around the epical story of the war between the Russians and Tartars, includes some Oriental elements, particularly in the musical characterization of the Tartars.

Moussorgsky, the most unprofessional of the Mighty Five, had the most genius. He served as a minor clerk in a government office, and began to compose very late in life. Besides, he indulged in a drinking habit far beyond the capacity of even his sturdy nature, and died as a result of an alcoholic ailment a week after his forty-second birthday. Most of his works were edited by his associate and friend, Rimsky-Korsakov. It is only recently that Moussorgsky's original scores have been published, and a comparison shows that often Moussorgsky anticipated modern harmonies which Rimsky-Korsakov had carefully corrected. Wrong harmonies of yesterday are modern chords of today. Moussorgsky's masterpiece is his opera, *Boris Godunov,* which pictures the tragic life of a Russian Czar who ascended the throne through the murder of a royal prince. The scene in which Boris Godunov sees the vision of the murdered boy is a psychological musical drama of remarkable realism.

Rimsky-Korsakov was a marine officer and served on a Russian cruiser that was an early Russian visitor in New York harbor. Like his associates of the Mighty Five, he acquired the science of musical composition with little formal study. Russia's colorful past particularly attracted his attention, and his operas present a wonderful panorama of Russian life, Russian song, and Russian legend.

The Mighty Five lived and composed music in the Czarist capital of Russia, St. Petersburg. Composers of Moscow pursued a more romantic style. There was Tchaikovsky, the unhappy genius, whose life was a series of misfortunes, and who poured out his pessimism into his symphonies, symphonic poems, and songs. In his diary, which he kept faithfully for many years, Tchaikovsky described his dreams, in which he always saw himself in dreadful peril, clinging to a jagged rock overhanging the ocean shore, or being pursued by implacable enemies. In his last composition, the *Pathétique Symphony,* Tchaikovsky introduced a theme from the Russian Mass for the Dead as a premonition of his fate. It was prophetic, for shortly after conducting the first performance of his Symphony, Tchaikovsky fell ill of cholera, and died a few days afterwards.

Very close to Tchaikovsky in spirit was Rachmaninoff, who wrote highly emotional music on such mournful subjects as the *Isle of the. Dead,* inspired by the German painting of a sepulchral island, with motionless cypress trees standing watch over the dead, and a boat with a human figure clad in white approaching the fateful shores. The last twenty-five years of his life, Rachmaninoff spent in America. He continued to compose, but his best and most enduring music was the product of early years—the Second Piano Concerto, which is played by pianists all over the world, his Piano Preludes, his romantic symphonies, and his passionate songs.

❧29❧

Musicians in Paris

NOT all great men of music were Germans. The towering achievement of Bach and Handel left sufficient space under the sun for their contemporaries in other nations. In Italy, there were Vivaldi and Scarlatti. In France, there were Couperin and Rameau. But the Latin temperament did not press in the direction of mountainous fugues and majestic oratorios. Vivaldi wrote fine instrumental music, which Bach knew and valued; Scarlatti composed delightful clavichord music. Rameau wrote entertaining suites, in which he represented such subjects as Sighs, the Lame Lady, the Hen, and gave a whole album of feminine characters: the Indifferent One, the Irritating One, the Timid One, the Indiscreet One, and the Stormy One. His delicate and charming *Tambourin* enjoys perennial popularity.

Rameau's older contemporary, François Couperin, was celebrated as an organ player as well as the composer of brilliant keyboard pieces. He was surnamed Le Grand to distinguish him from thirteen other Couperins, his close relatives, among them four women composers.

After Napoleon, Paris became the world's center of fashion, art and music. Musicians from all over Europe flocked to the City of Light to present their talents for the judgment of the discriminating Paris public. The Conservatory of Paris enjoyed a great reputation for learning. It was presided over by the stern-faced, strict Italian musician, Cherubini. Commercial music publishers offered opportunities to any composer who could attract the public fancy. Luxurious concert halls featured appearances by famous virtuosi. There was Paganini, demon of the violin; there were Italian singers idolized by the public. The Paris Opera staged magnificent productions. Rossini, the Italian composer, settled in Paris, where he produced his famous opera, *William Tell*. But the greatest visitors to Paris were two pianist-composers, Chopin and Liszt.

Chopin was born in Poland. His name is spelled in the Polish language, Szopen, but his father was a native of France. To Chopin himself, Poland and France were equally dear. He left Poland with the memory of an unfortunate love; he went to Paris for a career as a pianist and incidentally he began to compose. In Paris he met the emancipated woman novelist who wrote fiction under a man's name, George Sand. Chopin's soul was deeply wounded when George Sand published a novel in which she gave a fictional portrait of Chopin as a capricious and unmanageable genius. That led to a break, and separation. He was weakened by tuberculosis and died before reaching his fortieth birthday. There is an early daguerrotype of Chopin which represents him sitting in the reading room (there are books on the shelves), attired in a long coat, according to the fashion, with a large bow tie around the white collar. His large, broad forehead is framed with locks of long, black, wavy hair. The sunken eyes show fatigue and illness, and the sensitive mouth reflects suffering. Chopin's hands are crossed on his knees, and a bound volume of music lies near to his elbow.

Chopin wrote only piano music, but his piano writing had all the richness and color of a full orchestra. Classical composers for piano confined themselves to the barest indications of forte and piano, loud and soft, with an occasional crescendo. Chopin introduced into his piano compositions a scale of graduated nuances, subtle expression marks. He embroidered his writing with pearly passagework, chromatically embellished scales, and imaginative cadenzas. He wrote concert waltzes and sonatas; nocturnes and polonaises; preludes and concertos; and four piano compositions in a new form of a Ballade. Chopin's music conquered the musical world at once, and with all the changing fashions, it has not suffered eclipse during the entire century since his death.

Liszt was born a year later than Chopin, in Hungary (the word Liszt means flour in Hungarian). His musical abilities as a child were extraordinary. At eleven, he played piano in Vienna, where Beethoven heard him, and kissed him on the forehead after the performance. Liszt took lessons with Czerny, the author of the famous piano exercises familiar to all piano students. At the age of twelve, he arrived in Paris, which became his home for many years afterwards. Later he associated himself with Wagner, who married Liszt's daughter, Cosima. With Wagner, Liszt became known as the champion of the Music of the Future, which baffled and irritated academic musicians. They did not like Liszt's compositions, even though they admired his piano playing. Incidentally, Liszt was the first to use the word "recital" for a concert, because the word recital conveyed the meaning of a narrative, an address, and implied a more intimate communication between the musician and his audience. Liszt was also the first great virtuoso of the piano capable of evoking torrents of sonority from the instrument. Liszt's own Hungarian rhapsodies, his Concertos, and his enormously difficult Etudes, converted a pianist into a prestidigitator who had to do the work of twenty fingers with only ten.

Liszt was the pioneer of modern piano playing in the virtuoso manner. The race of prodigious piano players that arose after Liszt has such giants as Anton Rubinstein, who could make the piano murmur, whisper, or roar; Paderewski whose singing tone and impetuous temperament conquered the public of both hemispheres; Busoni who could interweave criss-crossing contrapuntal voices as if his fingers were separate instruments; and in our own day, Vladimir Horowitz whose fantastic technique converts the piano into an eighty-eight-piece orchestra.

The music of Liszt is program music in the sense that his compositions represent definite pictures, moods, or states of mind. Even more definitely programmatic was Hector Berlioz, to whom musical composition was often the means of expressing personal emotion. He wrote a symphony, *An Episode from the Life of an Artist,* as a musical message for Miss Smithson, an English actress with whom Berlioz was in love, and who later became his wife. Berlioz liked grandiose effects, and once conducted a gigantic concert which included a vocal quartet sung by eighty voices, an aria accompanied by eighty harps, and other such Brobdingnagian presentations. Like Liszt and Wagner, Berlioz was caricatured by cartoonists and mocked as a musician of the future. Years have passed, the passions have subsided. Liszt, Wagner, and Berlioz are long enshrined in music's hall of fame. It is now the turn of twentieth century modernists to suffer the attacks and derision of critics who profess sincere admiration for the "modernists" of the respectable past.

A CARTOON PUBLISHED IN NEW YORK (BY SCHIRMER) IN 1869, EN-
TITLED MUSIC OF THE FUTURE. THE INSCRIPTION BELOW SAYS:
WAGNER, NOT TO BE PLAYED MUCH TILL 1995.

⚘30⚘

The Modernists

WAGNER, Liszt, and Berlioz started a vogue for music of larger dimensions, more powerful sonority, and incidentally, longer duration. Wagner's operatic masterpiece, *The Ring of the Nibelung,* is a "festival played for three days and a preliminary evening," four operas in one, based on a connected story of the legendary magic ring. Richard Strauss, humorously nicknamed "Richard the Second" (Wagner was the first Richard, of course) applied Wagner's ideas to orchestral compositions, with a considerably increased dose of dissonance. He was attacked by the critics even more viciously than Wagner. Gustav Mahler developed the idea of Wagnerian "leading motives" in the direction of greater unity, and in his choral symphony, *The Song of the Earth,* used only three notes as the main theme for the entire work.

After Strauss and Mahler, came Arnold Schoenberg. In his music, he broke away entirely from traditional harmony, and declared that it was time to give major triads and other familiar chords a rest, and build new music on new foundations. Schoenberg's cadences repose on unresolved dissonances as blissfully as the Hindu fakir relaxes on a bed of protruding nails. In place of the old rules, Schoenberg established strict regulations of his own, the Technique of Twelve Tones. In this system, each theme is made up of twelve different notes, which are combined and recombined in the development of the composition. There are altogether 479,001,600 different combinations of twelve notes, and it would take a thousand years working on an eight-hour schedule a day writing a note every second to exhaust this number of possibilities!

For a time, it was the musical fashion to make music as complicated as possible. Ferruccio Busoni composed a piano work called *Fantasia Contrappuntistica,* with newfangled scales and arpeggios. The Hindu musician, Kaikhosru Sorabji, composed the longest piece for piano,

Opus Clavicembalisticum. It is 252 pages long and contains a theme with 44 variations, and another with 81 variations. It was performed only once, by the composer himself.

The most complicated orchestral work is *The Rite of Spring,* by the Russian modernist, Igor Stravinsky, which gives a panorama of pagan Russia of a thousand years ago. It was first performed in Paris as a ballet, with the great Russian dancer, Nijinsky, in the principal role. When the score was played in Boston, a listener who could not endure the sound and fury of Stravinsky's musical atom bomb, wrote his protest in verse to a Boston newspaper:

> Who wrote this fiendish Rite of Spring,
> What right had he to write the thing,
> Against our helpless ears to fling
> Its crash, clash, cling, clang, bing, bang, bing?
>
> And then to call it Rite of Spring,
> The season when on joyous wing
> The birds melodious carols sing
> And harmony's in everything!
>
> He who could write the Rite of Spring
> If I be right, by right should swing!

But Stravinsky's score is as gentle as a cooing dove in comparison with a composition by an Italian Futurist, Russolo, scored for a noise orchestra, including such instruments as Screamers, Screechers, Buzzers, Cracklers, Gurglers, Whisperers, Snorters, Splashers, Wheezers, and Roarers. When it was first presented in Paris, several people in the audience rushed to the stage, intending to beat up the noise musicians. But the Futurists were well trained in the art of boxing, as well as in the art of noises; as a result of the clash, several of the listeners had to be hospitalized, while the performers suffered no casualties to speak of.

In the early days of Soviet Russia, composers wrote ultra-modern music to match the idea of the modern state. The best known Soviet composer, Dmitri Shostakovitch, wrote an opera, *The Nose,* around a story about an army major whose nose mysteriously vanished while he was being shaved in a barbershop. Happily, it returned after a number of curious adventures. There are all sorts of unusual effects in the score, such as an orchestral sneeze, hiccoughs on the harp, and a chorus of eight janitors singing eight different advertisements. Shostakovitch has also written a symphony with a factory whistle in the score. But in his later symphonies, he has abandoned his youthful pranks in favor of melodic writing.

Prokofiev, the composer of the delightful symphonic fairy tale *Peter and the Wolf,* also indulged in some ultra-modern experiments, such as a Scherzo for four bassoons playing in different keys. But in his *Classical Symphony.* Prokofiev is almost as well-behaved as Haydn— almost, because he uses consecutive fifths and other terrible things forbidden by teachers.

Modern music in France never reached noisy extremes, owing to the Gallic sense of balance and moderation. Debussy was the composer of musical landscapes in subdued colors, and he used his dissonances with discretion. Yet his critics, brought up on old music, were outraged. "What a delightful succession of false relations!" wrote one of them; "What adorable progressions of consecutive triads, inevitably resulting in consecutive fifths and octaves! What a collection of dissonances, sevenths and ninths! No, I will never have anything to do with these musical anarchists!"

Debussy's comrade-in-arms of French modernism, Ravel, was also assailed by the critics. And yet, what can be more gentle than Ravel's music, his quiet *Pavane,* his enchanting symphonic picture, *La Valse?* And in his *Bolero,* Ravel uses only one theme and one harmony on C, but creates a kaleidoscope of tonal color by changing his instrumentation for every recurrence of the theme. No wonder Ravel has been called the Swiss watchmaker of modern music, so finely wrought are the little cogs and wheels of his scores.

The successors of Debussy and Ravel were the French composers known under the name of Les Six. Out of the six, only two have attained lasting importance in the musical world of today, Arthur Honegger and Darius Milhaud. Honegger's best known works are his symphonic locomotive, *Pacific 231,* and—in a quite different vein—a modern religious oratorio, *King David.* Darius Milhaud began as an *enfant terrible* of music, and composed a piece called *The Bull on the Roof,* in which most of the music was written simultaneously in two keys, C major and F sharp major. Then he, too, returned to a more classical type of musical composition, and to harmonies seasoned with moderate dissonance.

The name of Paul Hindemith stands high in modern music. He had to leave Germany, when Hitler and the Nazis inaugurated a campaign against all modern art, and he made his home in the United States. Hindemith's music is tense and powerful. It often wanders far away from the tonal center, but invariably comes home to roost.

Another German composer, Ernst Krenek, has also settled in the United States. As a young man of twenty-five, he created a sensation with his jazz opera, *Johnny Strikes Up the Band*. Later he turned to instrumental music composed in the technique of twelve tones.

Schoenberg and Stravinsky, too, are now in the United States as naturalized American citizens. Also in America is the Swiss-Jewish composer, Ernest Bloch, whose symphonic poem entitled *America* is a musical panorama of American history, from the pilgrims' landing to the jazz era. The great Hungarian modernist, Béla Bartók, came to America after his country fell into the hands of the Nazis, and died in New York. Several other men of modern music have come to this country to take part in the musical life of the New World. America has become the hub of the musical universe.

In the meantime, a whole generation of native-born composers arose in America to challenge the declining art of old Europe. MacDowell was the precursor of new American music. He lived and worked in New England and his poetic suites, *Woodland Sketches* and *New England Idyls,* reflect the atmosphere of the New England countryside. After MacDowell, a whole galaxy of composers arose in New England. Among them were Horatio Parker, the author of many effective choral compositions; Arthur Foote, the writer of poetic songs and character pieces; Frederick Converse, who glorified the automobile in his symphonic poem, *Flivver, 10,000,000;* George Chadwick, who wrote impeccable instrumental pieces and organ works; Henry Gilbert, whose music is American to the core and alive with accents of American life; Henry Hadley, the most cosmopolitan of the New England group; and the first American woman composer, Mrs. H. H. A. Beach.

All these New England composers belong to the past generation. They wrote American music with dignity and tradition, but their

America was still a colony of European music. American musicians of the twentieth century started off boldly in the cultivation of the modern American idiom. Geographically, too, they are not confined to America's window to Europe, the states of New England. There is Roy Harris, born in Oklahoma, whose music breathes the open air of the prairie. There is Aaron Copland, a native of Brooklyn, whose symphonic scores vibrate with the excitement of the American cities. There is Walter Piston, a native of Maine, who weaves American themes into a network of learned counterpoint; Howard Hanson of Wahoo, Nebraska, whose Americanism is tinged with the austere spirit of his Swedish ancestors; Roger Sessions, of New England ancestry, who writes absolute music in the modern contrapuntal style; George Antheil, the ultramodernist from New Jersey, who settled in Hollywood; Quincy Porter of Connecticut, the composer of well-sounding chamber music; William Schuman, who writes instrumental pieces in classical form with modern harmonies; Wallingford Riegger of Georgia, whose complex scores possess concentrated power; Edward Burlingame Hill, the New Englander who depicts the American scene in the musical palette of impressionistic colors; Carl Ruggles of Massachusetts, whose harmonies are surcharged with tense dissonance; Samuel Barber of Pennsylvania, composer of polished symphonic scores; John Alden Carpenter of Chicago, the businessman who likes to cultivate American contemporary themes; Deems Taylor of New York, the composer of melodious operas; Charles Wakefield Cadman of Pennsylvania, whose operas and symphonies are based on American subjects; Randall Thompson of New York, who writes symphonies and choral compositions in an effectively modernistic manner; Morton Gould of New York whose versatile talents include the composition of musical comedies as well as symphonic works; and Henry Cowell of California, the formidable modernist and inventor of "tone-clusters," played on the piano with forearms and fists.

A figure apart from the musical current is Charles Ives, the Connecticut Yankee, who long before the European modernists, wrote symphonic and instrumental music of astonishing originality. His works reflect the American scene in a series of striking musical tableaux. His *Concord Sonata* is probably the most difficult piano composition ever written; its four movements are the musical portraits of the great writers of Concord: Emerson, Hawthorne, the Alcotts, and Thoreau.

Every year, new names of American composers appear in music news. The most spectacular among these newcomers is Leonard Bernstein, born near Boston in 1918, who woke up one day to find himself famous, in his triple capacity as symphonic conductor, composer, and pianist. Not only does he conduct and compose serious music, but he is also proficient as the composer of popular songs and dances.

THE AMERICAN CONSERVATORY CIRCA 1890

(*from an old advertisement*)

31

Jazz, Swing, and Boogie Woogie

ON DECEMBER 23, 1938, history was made in the evolution of American musical folklore. On that date, two Negro pianists performed in Carnegie Hall, New York, a new type of popular music, called Boogie Woogie, playing four hands on two upright pianos. The word seems to be an Americanism of good standing, for there is an old expression "to pitch a boogie," which means to throw a party. Perhaps the best clue to the rhythmic nature of Boogie Woogie is furnished by the title of the most famous composition in that medium, *Beat Me Daddy, Eight to the Bar*. The eight beats to a bar in 4/4 time are pounded continuously in the bass, while the right hand supplies syncopation, or indulges in rhythmic counterpoint. The eight-to-the-bar bass is the classical Boogie Woogie beat.

In its brief existence Boogie Woogie has developed several other techniques. The bass may be in four beats, as in *Bearcat Crawl* or it may be in the form of a "Walking Bass," in syncopated octave intervals. The characteristic feature of Boogie Woogie is that here the Bass is the Boss. It determines not alone the rhythmic pattern, but also the harmony. This harmony is a succession of the tonic, subdominant, and dominant triads, with an occasional "blue" minor seventh thrown in.

Boogie Woogie is the latest development of Jazz. At first there was Ragtime, which was a syncopated American rhythm. Ragtime bands were extremely popular, and this popularity is reflected in Irving Berlin's song *Alexander's Ragtime Band*. Then came Jazz. Nobody knows who originated the word Jazz, and what it means, if anything. All we know is that the word was used for the first time in Chicago in 1916, when a news item was published in a theatrical trade magazine announcing the appearance of the "so-called Jazz Band." It is also known that the first Jazz Band played in New York in February 1917. Jazz bands instantly became popular. Soon they were playing overseas, in Paris, and after that the Jazz vogue spread like wildfire to the four corners of the earth. There is even a Russian Jazz orchestra in Moscow, though its playing is of the type that may be described by the lowbrow adjective, corny.

Jazz rhythms are, of course, typically American, but Jazz can be analyzed in highbrow terms as a development of the fourth species of counterpoint, which as we know, is syncopated counterpoint. There was a movie film in which a serious-minded professor of musical theory instructed his co-educational class in the mysteries of counterpoint. He gave his students a *"cantus firmus,"* that is, a theme to which a counterpoint is to be written. This theme was simply a C major scale. The moment the professor left the classroom, the Jazz-minded students sat at the piano and jazzed the counterpoint with plenty of rhythm. This contest between Counterpoint and Jazz is resolved when the professor himself catches the spirit and composes a Jazz Rhapsody which becomes a national best seller.

JAZZY COUNTERPOINT

Historically speaking, Jazz may be a development of the spiritual songs of the southern Negro. These Spirituals combine the simplicity of church hymns with the nervous rhythm of a Negro workingman. At any rate, Negro Spirituals lend themselves easily to Jazz rhythms. Also, the greatest performers of Jazz music are Negroes. Simultaneously with the development of Jazz music, there appeared sentimental chants known as Blues. The Negro composer, W. C. Handy, is to be credited with the creation of the first Blues. The original Blues came from a political campaign song which Handy wrote for an election in Memphis, Tennessee. It is probable that the Blues were influenced by the Negro Spirituals, and that Jazz in its turn was influenced by the Blues. This seems a pretty plausible pedigree.

When Jazz came of age, composers pounced upon it as a new source of inspiration. Even Ravel, visiting America, was tempted by Jazz rhythms, and used them in his Violin Sonata. But the composer who made real music out of Jazz was George Gershwin. His celebrated *Rhapsody in Blue* is, of course, the best example of symphonic Jazz, but he used Jazz with equal effect also in his Piano Concerto and in his Negro opera, *Porgy and Bess*. And his songs such as *I Got Rhythm* are the classics of popular Jazz.

After Jazz came Swing. Benny Goodman, recognized as the King of Swing, gives a learned description of Swing music as "collective improvisation, rhythmically integrated." This would come close to definitions of Hot Jazz. And Hot Jazz is, as the word implies, so many degrees Fahrenheit above Sweet Jazz, which is Jazz at room temperature.

Then there is a variety of Jazz music that is known as Jive. According to Cab Calloway's *Hepster's Dictionary* (Hepster is, of course, no misprint for Webster, but a hep cat, i.e., a swing musician), to jive means "to kid along, to blarney, stuff and things, also lingo or speech." The word Jive probably came from jibe, in the sense of agreeing, as in the phrase, "it does not jibe with your statements yesterday."

Jazz, Swing and Boogie Woogie are for better or worse the trademarks of American popular music. A story is told that when records of Swing music were played for the first time for the natives of a Pacific island, the listeners reacted to it with instinctive joy. This was their music, because it expressed the natural rhythm of the human body, which required no period of initiation. Perhaps this is the greatest compliment that Jazz music could receive.

32

Be Your Own Composer!

THE road to music is paved with hard cobblestones, which cause tears and tantrums in many a budding musician. No wonder that he or she will devise a million ways of dodging the music lesson. As the fateful hour strikes, the victim suddenly develops all kinds of occupational ailments—an itch, a thirst, a somnolence, or some other plausible complaint. But the little musicians-against-their-will have a large repertoire of their own pieces which they are willing to pound on the keys indefatigably for hours. The classic of the kiddies-on-the-keys is the celebrated *Chopsticks Waltz,* which has been described in the learned *Oxford Companion to Music* as "a quick waltz tune for the piano, four hands, performed by schoolgirls, as an amusement, in a traditional manner—the flat hand being held perpendicularly and the notes struck with its side, with a touch of glissando intercalated and dominant-tonic vamping in the bass part." Chopsticks is a universal masterpiece of cosmic origin—at least nobody knows when and how it was originated. But the tradition is honorable, and Liszt himself lent his hand to a set of variations on Chopsticks collectively composed by Rimsky-Korsakov, Borodin, and others.

Chopsticks confines its range to white keys. Another popular piece of children's piano repertoire, untaught, untutored, and unpublished, is played on the black keys, and has a verse to it:

> I love coffee, I love tea,
> I love the boys, and the boys love me.
> Tell your mother to hold her tongue.
> She had a beau when she was young.
> Tell your father just the same,
> For he was the one who changed her name.

Budding pianists dislike formal study, but are willing to play music if there is an element of a game. One such musical game which is both educational and acceptable to the child pianist is the Game of Sequences. A sequence in music is the repetition of a rhythmic pattern on different notes. Let the teacher play a musical theme based on the tonic triad in the right hand, in the high treble, and the accompaniment, four beats to a bar, in the left hand, in the middle register of the piano keyboard. Then the teacher changes to dominant harmony, and the pupil repeats the tune, also in the dominant key, down in the bass. If

I LOVE COFFEE, I LOVE TEA

the teacher plays C, E, G, then the child plays the Dominant triad, G, B, D. If the teacher plays G, A, and G, the pupil is to play D, E, and D. At the end both teacher and pupil play a musical signature which, of course, must end on the Tonic chord. If both the teacher and the pupil are exceptionally inventive, the original phrase may be embellished with chromatic passing notes and it may even take a plunge into atonal jazz music. The technique of Boogie Woogie is also adaptable to the Game of Musical Sequences.

Children who refuse to take their music lessons straight may be lured to the piano by devious means. For instance, a musically stubborn child may refuse to play scales and arpeggios, but will consent to practice with a pencil or a piece of paper placed on the strings so that the piano sounds like a tin pan. Incidentally, this effect has been treated quite seriously by John Cage, champion of percussion music in America, who composes special music for pianos with miscellaneous gadgets scattered over the strings. The expression, Tin Pan Alley, originated in a similar manner, from an upright piano converted into a tin pan by inserting bits of paper and nails between the strings. The late composer of popular songs, Von Tilzer, is credited with the invention of the original tin pan, as well as of the expression, Tin Pan Alley.

THE GAME OF MUSICAL SEQUENCES

Musical jokes may often break a path to music. Among conservatory students, an academic prank of ancient standing is the performance of Chopin's *Etude on the Black Keys* by rolling an orange, more or less in keeping with the rhythm and range of the right hand, and playing the accompaniment correctly with the left hand. In the same category belongs the execution of the *Tannhäuser Overture* with a whiskbroom, imitating the sound of the high violins in Wagner's score.

In music appreciation classes, one often hears this question: "How does a composer compose music?" Must he have inspiration from nature? Is it right to suppose that more good music is written in good weather? The answer is, no. Composers are professional craftsmen, and their technical ability enables them to produce music under any circumstances, in fair weather or foul, in a state of exalted joy, or in the depths of depression. Mozart, Haydn and Beethoven wrote some of their best music on commission from their wealthy friends in a businesslike way.

For many years, musicians have tried to devise methods for composing music mechanically. Kirnberger, a pupil of Bach, published a volume entitled *The Ready Composer of Minuets and Polonaises* which listed ready-made musical phrases that could be assembled into a musical piece by number system. Mozart, too, contrived a Musical Dice Game, with 176 separate bars of music on cards, and an index, showing the corresponding bar for each throw of dice.

It is possible to construct a slot machine that could turn out acceptable sets of variations and even fugues. The customer pushes buttons corresponding to the notes of the theme, pulls a few levers to indicate the rhythmic pattern, and a fugue, printed on a sheet of music paper, drops into a special tray. If the theme is unworkable, you get your nickel back.

Pending the invention of the Fugue Machine, here is a seemingly foolproof method of composing variations. The automatic composer is not expected to know anything about harmony or theory. In fact, he does not even have to read the notes. All he must do is follow these explicit instructions, and the result is guaranteed to satisfy

The notes of the melody in this system are contained within the range of an octave, from Dominant to Dominant. In the key of C Major, the melody will then include the notes G, A, B, C, D, E, F, G. It is recommended that the first note of the theme shall be C, E, or one of the two G's. The last note should be C, the Tonic. The number of bars shall be eight, with two notes to a bar, except the last bar, which will have only one note. The total number of the notes in the theme will then be fifteen, seven bars of two notes each, and one bar with one note.

The reason for the selection of this range for the theme is that the best folk songs, hymns and anthems are similarly constructed. Among specimens of such melodies are the *Marseillaise, Over There, Yankee Doodle,* and many other celebrated tunes. The analysis of such melodies will also show that the best melodic skips are along the Tonic and the Dominant triads.

The only chords to be used in this system of automatic composition are the Tonic, Subdominant, and the Dominant Seventh chord. C, E, and G will be harmonized by Tonic chords; F and A by the Subdominant; B and D by the Dominant Seventh. Lest a harmony teacher raise his eyebrows at the use of the Subdominant rather than the Dominant Seventh to harmonize F, there are reasons for doing so. The F in the Subdominant provides stronger harmony for a contrast with the Tonic and Dominant chords used in harmonizing most of the melodies.

These chords are always used in close harmony, and are played by the right hand on the piano. The left hand plays a fixed bass which is a pedal point on the Tonic and Dominant. In the key of C Major, this pedal point is C and G.

Variations are built from the theme according to the following patterns: (1) Chords in arpeggios going up or down; (2) long grace notes above the melody notes, as for instance, D resolving to C, or F resolving to E; (3) long grace notes a semitone below the melody note, as for instance, B resolving to C, and F Sharp resolving to G; (4) broken chords with grace notes, resulting in four-note figurations.

Further variations are obtained by using long grace notes in the middle voice of each chord, or in the bottom voice. It is amazing how musical such variations are, and how professional they sound. Rhythmic variety may be provided by making the grace note twice as long as the principal note, producing melodies in waltz time.

Each variation is rounded off with a coda, by repeating the last four bars of the variation, then the last two, then the last bar, and then the last half-bar twice, eight bars in all. Each succeeding section should be played softer and slower than the preceding one, which contributes a fading-out effect. These little tricks of trade are rather obvious, but great composers have not disdained to make use of them.

Of course, themes for variations may be written in minor keys. In this case, the seventh note of the scale must be raised. When the melody goes up by degrees from the Dominant to the Tonic, the sixth degree should be raised as well, making it a melodic minor scale. When descending from the Tonic to the Dominant, the natural minor scale may

be used. The effect of these changing chords in the three different
minor scales—natural, harmonic, and melodic—is truly remarkable.

BE YOUR OWN COMPOSER!

Double grace notes, too, may be used, provided they run in consecutive thirds and sixths, or in contrary motion. And triple notes, too. Such
triple embellishments lead us right into the realm of polytonality. For
instance, a triple embellishment, by semitones, of C major chords results in enharmonic G sharp minor chords; triple embellishments of
F major chords are enharmonic C sharp minor chords, and triple

embellishments of Dominant Seventh chords, in the key of C, are F sharp major chords. Over the fixed C-G Pedal Point, these harmonies create a fascinating bitonal effect.

Finally, our theme and variations can be arranged for instruments. Give the double pedal point to the cello. Have two violins play the upper two notes and give the lower note of the chord to the viola. Use muted strings, if you like soft music.

And now our automatic composer may proudly proclaim:

> **THEY LAUGHED AT ME**
>
> when I said I could compose beautiful music, but their laughter changed to amazement when I sat down at the piano and performed my Theme and Variations, op. 343.

Index